**Bibliografische Information der Deutschen Nationalbibliothek:**

Die Deutsche Nationalbibliothek verzeichnet diese Publikation in der Deutschen Nationalbibliografie; detaillierte bibliografische Daten sind im Internet über http://dnb.d-nb.de abrufbar.

**Impressum:**

Copyright © 2016 Studylab

Ein Imprint der GRIN Verlag, Open Publishing GmbH

Druck und Bindung: Books on Demand GmbH, Norderstedt, Germany

Coverbild: Freepik.com | Flaticon.com | GRIN

# Kinga Gmiat

# Trauma and Postmemory in Art Spiegelman's "The Complete Maus" and Helen Fremont's "After Long Silence"

2015

# 1.    Introduction

Research has shown that personal as well as collective trauma have a long-term effect on victims of genocides and catastrophes. Our society still tries to cope with the event which took place in the 20th century namely the massive homicide of approximately 6 million people of Jewish descent undertaken by the Nazi regime. Before World War II, 9 million Jews had lived across Europe, whereas only 7 years later 90% of them have been either gassed, burned or shot (cf. Epstein 1987, p. 11). Not only does the generation that witnessed and survived the Holocaust deal with its bodily and psychic consequences even seventy years later, but also the generation after, the so called "second generation" receives more and more attention in the scholarly field of Holocaust studies.

"One may observe that the Shoah is an extreme instance of a traumatic series of events that pose the problem of denial or disavowal, acting-out, and working-through" (LaCapra 1994, p. 187). The Holocaust depicts an event of such magnitude and such an absurd reality that even victims back then could not imagine or comprehend its magnitude (cf. ibid., p. 220).

The Holocaust represents a historical as well as a cultural trauma. Members of a collectivity acknowledge they have been subjected to a horrific event and traumatic situation, which scars their group consciousness and their memories forever. Groups take on social responsibility and political action (cf. Alexander: *Toward a Theory of Cultural Trauma*. In: *Cultural Trauma and Collective Identity*. 2004, p. 1). A trauma is a social construct, which defines a collectivity as a victim and the enemy as a perpetrator (cf. ibid., p. 10). Traumata are continuously and culturally reproduced via monuments, rituals and commemorations. The representations of traumata reproduce and shape collective identity (cf. ibid., pp. 22-23).

Historical trauma is always related to certain events that include losses. Massive loss of life due to murder in ghettos and in concentration camps ruled everyday life during the Holocaust. Communities were destroyed and masses exterminated (cf. Kirmayer/Gone/Moses 2014, p. 304). Historical traumata as the Shoah can be located and its temporality determined (cf. LaCapra 2001, pp. 81-82). The notion of historical trauma suggests also that its event has a negative impact on individuals which poses problems for later generations involving intergenerational transmission of trauma (cf. ibid., p. 307). The trauma of the first generation has therefore consequences for their children, to whom the trauma is transferred and which is to be specified as the concept of postmemory.

Hirsch defines the term "postmemory" in her work *The Generation of Postmemory* and discusses the transfer of first generation memory, particularly the memory of the Holocaust, to the second generation. She defines the term as a relationship of the second generation to traumatic experiences, which occurred before their births and which have been transmitted to them so intensively that they seem to have become their own memories. Descendants of survivors who lived through traumatic events are able to connect deeply to the experiences and the remembrance of the first generation. Nevertheless, the received and transmitted memories are different from those of the witnesses.

The following thesis talks about the trauma symptoms and the behavior of Holocaust victims. In chapter 2, the specific feature of prolonged trauma victims will be examined due to the ongoing mental and physical abuse during the Holocaust and the possibilities for a successful recovery are going to be depicted. The examination will base its claims on the works of scholars as Cathy Caruth, Dominik LaCapra, Judith Herman, Sigmund Freud and Dori Laub. Caruth´s accentuation on an unspeakable truth of the trauma and her portrayal of survivor guilt as well as Herman´s focus on possible symptoms of trauma victims will contribute to the work considerably. The term "Shoah" and "Holocaust" will be used interchangeably.

In chapter 4, the concept of postmemory and the way survivor children deal with the impact of their parents´ trauma will be based on Marianne Hirsch´s definition of this term and other second generation authors as Eva Hoffman and Helen Epstein, who both incorporated their own experiences of familial transmission of trauma as well as those of their interviewees in their works. Afterwards, features of postgeneration art will be presented in detail.

Second generation literature and art mirrors the depression and horrid state of the mind of survivors. Art Spiegelman´s *The Complete MAUS*, which is divided into two parts, "My father bleeds history" and "And here my troubles began", will be analyzed as a whole. Before looking at features of trauma theory in chapter 3 as well as the concept of postmemory in chapter 5, the specific characteristics of comics will be pointed out at first. The work is a white-black comic, which talks about a father´s past before, during and after World War II. Spiegelman describes his father´s traumatic experiences during the war as well as his inability of coping with those after it. Additionally, the implied author, whom is going to be referred to as Art, depicts his own feelings and emotions concerning his father´s past and the way his father´s trauma affects his own life.

In chapter 6, another second generation piece will be analyzed within the context of trauma as well as postmemory theory. In Helen Fremont´s memoir *After Long Silence* the implied author describes the lives of her parents, survivors of World War II, before, during and after the war. Raised as a Roman Catholic, Helen discovers her parents´ Jewish descent as an adult and starts exploring her family´s real identity as well as her own after many years of silence.

In both works the first generation deals with the effects of World War II and its aftermath. The thesis aims at portraying the degree of traumatization as well as the extent to which the second generation is affected by the traumatic experiences of the parents´ lives. The questions that are going to be answered in the thesis are the following: How does the intergenerational transmission of memory take place? What do the children do to inscribe themselves into the stories of their parents in order to find their own identity on the voyage of discovery of the past? To what extent are the children affected by postmemory?

The topic about trauma theory and the concept of postmemory is especially interesting since it offers a depiction of the characters´ behavior in two different genres, a comic and a memoir. In conclusion, both works will be compared and their differences and similarities depicted.

The thesis might contribute to a successful ongoing remembering of the Holocaust and its aftermath. The topic of the Shoah and its aftermath increases in academic fields more and more. Its consequences on the psyche are not yet fully captured. Since not only the first generation is implicated in it, but also the following generation, the topic of the Holocaust continues on to this day. It is going to persist as long as people, who are either directly or indirectly touched by its effects, decide to commemorate the memories of their ancestors.

## 2. Psychological Trauma

### 2.1 Symptoms and Behavior

Traumatic stress studies include a large amount of areas, as post-traumatic stress disorder studies or Nazi Holocaust studies, in which the: "[...] investigation of the immediate and long term psychosocial consequences of highly stressful events [...]" (Figley: *Foreword*. In: *Human Adaptation to Extreme Stress. From the Holocaust to Vietnam.* 1988, p. ix) takes place and the criterions that affect these consequences are analyzed (cf. ibid.). There is a wide variety on traumatic disorders, reaching from the aftereffects of a single event to prolonged and re-peated violence (cf. Herman 1997, p. 3). The psychiatrist and professor Judith Herman claims: "To study psychological trauma is to come face to face with human vulnerability in the natural world and with the capacity for evil in human nature" (ibid., p. 7). Those who bear witness are doing this to terrible events and it is impossible to behave in a neutral manner (cf. ibid.).

Psychological trauma constitutes the outcome of stressful events that demolish a victim´s sense of security and makes him feel helpless and isolated (cf. ibid., p. 197). A person is considered a victim as soon as he is subjected to a human per-petrator (cf. Rothe 2011, p. 25). We are dealing with atrocities when humans constitute the overwhelming force that traumatizes people (cf. Herman 1997, p. 33). Every person reacts differently to a traumatic occurrence (cf. ibid., p. 58). Usually, the reaction to violence and atrocities that people suffering from post-traumatic stress disorder or PTSD undergo, is to eliminate them from conscious-ness (cf. Caruth 1996, p. 11) since trauma symbolizes a sore place in a person´s psyche, which hurts incredibly when it is being touched (cf. Fischer 1989, p. 18).

The term *trauma* derives from the Greek word for "wound", which originally referred invariably to an injured body. The philosopher and psychoanalyst Sig-mund Freud discovered at the end of the 19th century that trauma has not only physical effects, but also an impact on the victim´s or a patient´s mind (cf. Hirsch 2004, p. 8). Trauma refers to a subjective suffering that weakens and shatters the individual´s mental apparatus (cf. Freud 1923, pp. 9-10). The victim is not able to remember all the details of a traumatic situation and suppresses these, which leads to a re-emergence of those. The victim, being focused on his trauma (cf. ibid., p. 11), is occupied by a repetition compulsion, in

which the suppressed resurfaces repeatedly (cf. ibid., p. 20). The repetitive repression, taking place in the unconsciousness, illustrates unwanted reproductions, which have not been turned into memories yet (cf. ibid., pp. 20-21).

The mind is not able to communicate the impressions of the traumatic incident into a coherent and continuous psychological representation. What remains are unprocessed, unassimilated impressions that stay in the mind (cf. Hirsch 2004, p. 15). At the same time, those untreated memories stay with the victim: "Paradoxically, they neither submit to the normal processes of memory storage and recall, nor, returning uninvited, do they allow the event to be forgotten" (ibid., pp. 15-16).

What inevitably goes along with this reaction of banishing memories from the consciousness, is the unspeakability of those violations and the impossibility of uttering those experiences aloud (cf. Herman 1997, p. 1). The professor Cathy Caruth claims that trauma is: "[...] the moving and sorrowful voice that cries out, a voice that is paradoxically released through the wound" (Caruth 1996, p. 2). There is an otherness of a voice which witnessed a truth the victim is not able to fully comprehend yet. This voice tries to tell the sufferer of an unimaginable and impalpable truthfulness and veracity (cf. ibid., p. 3). The traumatic experience is "[...] experienced too soon, too unexpectedly, to be fully known and is therefore not available to consciousness until it imposes itself again [...]" (ibid., p. 4). The obtrusion can take the form of nightmares or repeated actions (cf. ibid.).

There is the possibility of linking one´s own trauma to that of another. Hearing a voice in another human being, which speaks through the wound, and listening to it may offer an encounter with that other person and getting in touch with his and one´s own trauma simultaneously (cf. ibid., p. 8).

The trauma´s nature is unassimilated in the victim´s past and cannot be simply located in its original event. It cannot be known and, as this unknown instance, possesses the victim at a later date (cf. ibid.). Trauma reflects "[...] always the story of a wound that cries out, that addresses us in the attempt to tell us of a reality or truth that is not otherwise available" (ibid.) Not only is the truth of the trauma characterized by a delayed response, but it also has to be linked to what remains unknown and unsaid in actions as well as in language (cf. ibid.). PTSD mirrors the direct mental burden of an inevitable reality of terrible events that is not controllable (cf. ibid., p. 58).

Judith Herman presents the concept of a central dialectic of psychological trauma stating that there are two tendencies that victims of PTSD have a disposition to. On the one hand they feel the need to deny their experiences and distract their audience from listening to them. On the other hand there is the will to proclaim their past aloud and call attention to it. Both tendencies work at the same time (cf. Herman 1997, p. 1). Testimonies are often given in an emotional and fragmented manner and they are full of contradictories, which undermine the speaker´s credibility (cf. ibid.). The desire to keep the experience a secret usually prevails. The story of a traumatic situation or event emerges thus as a symptom and not as a narrative. However, victims still oscillate between the desire to tell and to keep their trauma a secret, so they also oscillate between the condition of feeling numb and reliving the whole experience again (cf. ibid.).

Victims of PTSD have difficulties seeing more than a few fragments of the whole image at one time that constitutes their experience. They feel overwhelmed when trying to put all the pieces together and make them fit. What is even more challenging for them is finding language and speaking publicly about it. Most of the time, the tendency to deny and repress prevails (cf. ibid., p. 2).

Psychological trauma involves episodic amnesia. Periods of oblivion replace investigations of the past and vice versa (cf. ibid., p. 7). Trauma overwhelms the human adaptations to life. They include encounters with death and violence as well as threats to life that make the victims feel overpowered by helplessness and terror (cf. ibid., p. 33). The threat to life may be either sudden or introduced step by step. The dimension of a traumatization due to a threat or end to life depends on the victim´s degree of unacceptability of and vulnerability to it (cf. Lifton: *Understanding the Traumatized Self. Imagery, Symbolization, and Transformation.* In: *Human Adaptation to Extreme Stress. From the Holocaust to Vietnam.* 1988, p. 19). Powerlessness captures the person concerned and an overwhelming force breaks down an ordinary system of care that assures a sense of control, connection, and meaning (cf. Herman 1997, p. 33).

During the moment of danger the human system of reactions engages the body and the mind. Threat arouses the nervous system and causes the victim to feel adrenalin rushing through his body, which makes him go into a condition of alert. The person focuses on the dangerous situation that he is in. In this condition, the person is able to ignore pain, tiredness or hunger. He is forced to stay focused on exhausting actions as fighting or battling, which will eventually raise his will to survive. When this kind of action is not profitable anymore and the human system of self-defense is overpowered, a traumatic reaction sets in (cf. ibid., p. 34).

As a result, people with PTSD may see long lasting and profound changes in arousal, cognition and emotion. Memory may be effected. Intense emotions may be experienced without a precise memory of a traumatizing event or the other way around, so that victims have an emotionless detailed memory of everything that happened (cf. ibid.). Another possibility is suffering amnesia for the life before an event or crime as the Holocaust. Many survivors have an erased memory of their lives before the trauma (cf. Danieli: *Confronting the Unimaginable. Psychotherapist´s Reactions to Victims of the Nazi Regime*. In: *Human Adaptation to Extreme Stress*. 1988, p. 221).

The traumatized person may feel constantly vigilant and irritated without knowing the reason for this behavior (cf. Herman 1997, p. 34). Symptoms that evolve due to a traumatic event are cut off from the source since trauma fragments the complicated system of self-protection. The human nervous system is separated from the present and victims of PTSD act due to that state. They behave as if they were still in a dangerous and traumatic situation in their past and cut off from the present (cf. ibid., pp. 34-35).

The historian Dominick LaCapra differentiates between two reciprocal processes that a victim undergoes. Regardless of their linking, those are still distinguishable and sometimes counteracting procedures (cf. LaCapra 2001, p. 71). On the one hand he pays attention to "acting out", an action, in which the patient relives the traumatic event. It haunts the victim and re-emerges as the repressed (cf. ibid., p. 70). Acting out implies repetition compulsion and the inability to gain distance from the traumatic situation. The victims then relives the past in the present. Flashbacks and nightmares may set in (cf. ibid., pp. 142-143). When loss and absence merge and are not kept apart, melancholic paralysis may occur (cf. ibid., p. 64) and the process of acting out, which involves melancholia and the unwillingness to accept one´s loss (cf. LaCapra 1994, p. 209), may perhaps hinder the overcoming of trauma (cf. ibid., p. 205). Acting out may be closely tied to "working through" and even be necessary to make the latter possible (cf. ibid., p. 208). Working through on the other hand contains the victim´s ability to distinguish past and present and keep them separated. The patient understands that something happened in the past, but knows it is not related in any sense to the present he lives in now (cf. LaCapra 2001, p. 66). In this case the possibility of mourning is given. The person suffering from trauma remembers the trauma in a performative way and tries to forget and accept it at the same time (cf. ibid., p. 70). He is opened for argumentative judgement, a self-questioning (cf. La-Capra 1994, p. 210) and a new way of living including social norms and empathy for other people, which was not possible before (cf. LaCapra 2001, p. 70). The difference between absence and loss is understood and the process of mourning may start (cf. ibid., pp. 46-47).

As soon as a trauma becomes stored as a memory and "[...] when language functions to provide some measure of conscious control, critical distance, and perspective, one has begun the arduous process of working over and through the trauma [...]" (ibid., p. 90). Working through is a preferable action and it permits incorporating trauma in one´s own life (cf. ibid., pp. 143-144).

The most complex issue with working through is the ability to accept trauma and to always go back trying to work it over without the feeling of betraying the people one lost during the traumatic event. The trust and love that binds a victim to the people he lost may cause the patient to stick with trauma in order to keep fidelity with them. The patient needs to comprehend that his working through does not make him forget the dead eventually (cf. ibid., p. 144). A controlled life-changing process of repetition that working through presents makes a selective scanning of the past possible (cf. LaCapra 1994, p. 174). The future is not blocked anymore and the grieving that the victim suffers from diminishes (cf. LaCapra 2001, p. 151). Acting out and working through demonstrate not a relationship, in which one develops and becomes the other (cf. LaCapra 1994, p. 205), but a combination, in which both are never completely separate from one another (cf. LaCapra 2001, p. 150).

Herman proposes three main categories, in which the symptoms of PTSD fall into. She speaks of hyperarousal, intrusion and constriction. People who fall into the first category anticipate a return of the danger any time after a traumatic occurrence: "The traumatized person startles easily, reacts irritably to small provocations, sleeps poorly" (Herman 1997, p. 35). He behaves aggressively and explosively (cf. ibid.).

When people with PTSD deal with intrusion, they relive the unsafe situation they have experienced, which all of the sudden comes back into consciousness in nightmares or as flashbacks during daily activities. Any circumstances, conversations or material things may remind them of the original occurrence and memories may be brought back (cf. ibid., pp. 37-38.) Even sounds or smells might remind a victim of his trauma (cf. Fischer 2008, p. 20). Those memories, which repetitively emerge, are non-linear and cannot be put into language or an on-going narrative (cf. Herman 1997, pp. 37-38). The emotions that were involved during the original traumatic incident recur with the same intensity (cf. ibid., p. 42). The victim is controlled by terror and rage, which constitute an enormous emotional distress and from which survivors tend to retreat. This makes the condition of PTSD worse, which again leads to a withdrawal from engagement with other people (cf. ibid., p. 42).

When the system of self-defense completely crashes and the feeling of helplessness prevails, the victim is situated in a condition of constriction. The person´s state of consciousness changes and he surrenders. His perceptions may be distorted and he feels an emotional distance and indifference (cf. ibid., p. 43). The quality of a victim´s life is diminished: "In avoiding any situations reminiscent of the past trauma, or any initiative that might involve future planning or risk, traumatized people deprive themselves of those new opportunities for successful coping that might mitigate the effect of the traumatizing experience" (ibid., p. 47).

A survivor finds himself between the extreme points of amnesia and re-experiencing a trauma. He finds himself in a condition of instability (cf. ibid., pp. 47-48).

When a victim is traumatized, he suffers from a disconnection, which unsettles the construction of himself (cf. ibid., p. 51). Trauma however has not only effects on the psyche of the person concerned but also on the human relationships he has with others. Disconnection violates relations with family members, friends, partners and the community in general (cf. ibid., p. 49). The primary effects of trauma are one´s own shattered psychological structures and the bonding that connect community and the individual person. Once the trust in a safe environment, shelter as well as comfort do no longer exist, the victim feels abandoned and lonely, which leads to a disconnection (cf. ibid., pp. 51-52). He is left with shame and doubt and has to re-establish his lost sense for autonomy, identity and intimacy (cf. ibid., pp. 52-53). Due to a disturbed sense of a normal meaningful world, the survivor is not able to modulate deep anger and lives out intolerance and expressions of rage. These outbursts of fury may turn against strangers as well as family members (cf. ibid., pp. 54-56). This instable behavior leads to a withdrawal from intimate relationships due to a feeling of shame and guilt as well as a breakdown in trust. A wish for a protective environment and a need for close relationships with people are nevertheless wished for by survivors. Traumatized people alternate between isolation and withdrawal and an urge for intimacy at the same time (cf. ibid, p. 56).

Caruth mentions an oscillation between the "crisis of death" and the "crisis of life", which she calls the "double telling". Having experienced an event or situation that involves the threat of death implies also the aspect of survival. Those two conditions are inseparable regardless of their apparent incompatibility (cf. Caruth 1996, p. 8).

The victim partly feels a relief after his survival. He also feels shame and guilt because of having survived the experience when others have not. The feelings of joy due to the own survival may in fact and paradoxically cause additional guilt in survivors (cf. Lifton: *Understanding the Traumatized Self. Imagery, Symboli-*

*zation, and Transformation.* In: *Human Adaptation to Extreme Stress. From the Holocaust to Vietnam.* 1988, p. 21). Survivor guilt may be expressed in many ways. It may appear as a feeling of self-doubt, shame or a responsibility for the death of other people (cf. Williams: *Diagnosis and Treatment of Survivor Guilt: The Bad Penny Syndrome.* In: *Human Adaptation to Extreme Stress. From the Holocaust to Vietnam.* 1988, p. 321).

People, who listen to survivor stories or read testimonies of traumatic occurrences, may also be effected by trauma. The listener becomes a participant of the traumatic event and to some extent experiences trauma himself. The relation the victim has to his own trauma influences the listener´s relation to it. The listener may feel confusion, dread or bewilderment and all the emotions that the victim feels. There is also the possibility of feeling the survivor´s victories, silences and defeats. However, he does not become the victim since he is a separate individual who stays in his own place and keeps his perspective while hearing the stories. The emotions he feels may nevertheless rage within, so he is not only a witness to the survivor, but also a witness to himself (cf. Laub: *Bearing Witness, or the Vicissitudes of Listening.* In: Felman/Laub: *Testimony. Crises of Witnessing in Literature, Psychoanalysis, and History.* 1992, pp. 57-58). The "vicarious traumatization" that takes place then, has its origins in the clinical context, in which it describes helping another person situated in front of one as it is the case with therapists and patients. The term however can be applied to readers, listeners and viewers who are also affected by the survivor´s stories (cf. Kaplan 2005, pp. 122-123). Other survivors may also be influenced by the stories of different victims. Survivors, who already experienced a traumatic situation, are very sensitive and more susceptible to go through a new trauma and be controlled by the emotions of another speaker: "If the traumata are not dealt with, understood, and put into perspective, additional stress accumulate more easily" (Williams: *Diagnosis and Treatment of Survivor Guilt: The Bad Penny Syndrome.* In: *Human Adaptation to Extreme Stress. From the Holocaust to Vietnam.* 1988, p. 321).

Victims of severe and prolonged trauma are especially delicate and sensitive due to the massive impact on their psyche. The specific nature of such trauma victims and their extreme conditions of chronic abuse and prolonged trauma will be portrayed in the next chapter.

## 2.2   Prolonged Trauma and Captivity

Prolonged or repeated trauma takes place in situations in which people are imprisoned or held in captivity. Any possibilities of an escape are eliminated or restricted and the victims are controlled by perpetrators at all times. This kind of captivity takes place in concentration camps, in which the victim has continuing contact with the perpetrator (cf. Herman 1997, p. 74). The survivor is constantly confronted with physical violence and emotional terror. The perpetrator keeps him in permanent fear and threatens his life on a daily basis. The belief in an almighty perpetrator is always present and resistance is regarded as impossible (cf. ibid., p. 77). The survivor´s sense of autonomy is degraded by an immense force: "Fear also increased by inconsistent and unpredictable outbursts of violence and by capricious enforcement of petty rules" (ibid.).

The abuser is always in control of the victim´s body. By isolating him from his family, friends and a familiar environment he makes him dependent since he is the only person the victim has contact with (cf. ibid., pp. 80-81). When the victim relinquishes his own autonomy and gives up his urge to survive, his psyche is broken. When the prisoner surrenders and does not want to live anymore, he is dominated by passivity and internally broken completely (cf. ibid., pp. 84-85).

It is the recurrence of the experience that survivors of chronic abuse dread the most. They reveal mostly hyperarousal symptoms (cf. ibid., p. 86) that put the victim into a constant state of alert. Survivors of captivity and concentration camps show no physical calm or ease. They have difficulties getting sleep and complain frequently about somatic symptoms as: "[...] tension headaches, gastro intestinal disturbances and abdominal back, or pelvic pain [...]" (ibid.). The trauma they suffer from is linked to the bodily stress they undergo after their survival (cf. ibid).

Other symptoms survivors of repeated or the so called complex trauma (cf. ibid., p. 158) suffer from are those of intrusion, in which victims live out the traumatic event as if it was in the present. They may fade away some time after acute trauma, but they have effects in the long run when it comes to chronic trauma patients. The most typical characteristics with chronic trauma patients is avoidance or constriction, in which they suppress activities, relationships, emotions and sensations (cf. ibid., p. 87).

The moment, in which a prisoner learns to think in terms of a constriction, may already be when he is in captivity. The thought of a possible future can be too unbearable to think of. That is why by surrendering to constriction he protects himself from the vulnerability of being deeply disappointed (cf. ibid., pp. 86-88). According to Herman, it is extremely difficult to incorporate repeated trauma of a long-term captivity into a victim´s life story (cf. ibid., p. 89). If a person shies away from denying his experience, the suffering only worsens: "The more the period of captivity is disavowed [...] the more this disconnected fragment of the past remains fully alive [...]" (ibid.).

Prevalent for survivors of prolonged trauma is the urge to handle daily tasks with a special ingenuity and determination. Thinking about survival, which was present during captivity, still exists even during daily responsibilities after the event. While focusing on survival, victims unlearn the capability of managing easy tasks since they were not allowed to undertake them in captivity. Victims have the feeling of being overstrained by little things and duties (cf. ibid., p. 90), but they leave no room for mistakes neither for others nor for themselves: "Prolonged captivity undermines or destroys the ordinary sense of a relatively safe sphere of initiative, in which there is some tolerance for trial and error" (ibid., p. 91).

In prolonged trauma the victims seem to be unable to imagine a different world from the violent one they know or to question the brutal environment they are in (cf. Baer 2002, pp. 21-22). They are controlled by the rules of this world completely. People suffering from a repeated trauma question the issue of trust in every person they meet even after survival. They know a limited number of roles ranging from the perpetrators, passive witnesses, rescuers and allies and apply those to the people they encounter after. Every relationship is analyzed within the context of these roles (cf. Herman 1997, p. 92). If a patient regards another person as a perpetrator and puts him in this category, he will have the tendency to flee from that person. If he considers a person to be a rescuer, he will stick to him and value this relationship. These roles are not necessarily maintained for a longer period of time. They may change all of the sudden at all times. If a patient is disappointed by a person he or she trusts, the applied role may change and the wrongdoer be downgraded to a role of a perpetrator or accomplice (cf. ibid., p. 93).

The isolation the victim feels after the traumatic situation is due to the impossibility of pleasing him, since most people fail the test of trustability imposed by the patient. Because of the victim´s disappointment in others he sticks to solitude (cf. ibid., p. 93).

Chronic trauma causes permanent changes in personality and alters the survivor´s psyche for the rest of his life: "People subjected to prolonged, repeated trauma develop an insidious, progressive form of post-traumatic stress disorder that invades and erodes the personality" (ibid., p. 86). People who lived through a single traumatic event may also be shattered and feel a change in their personality. Repeated trauma however changes a person irrevocably and makes him feel as if he completely lost his identity (cf. ibid., pp. 84-85).

The effects of a chronic trauma experience on a victim´s personality is of long duration, most often until his death. The person that the patient was before his captivity does no longer exist. His identity has changed and cannot be re-established after a release: "Whatever new identity she develops in freedom must include the memory of her enslaved self" (ibid.).

The mental scars of prolonged trauma that victims have continue to exist long after the rescue. Not only are they afflicted with post-traumatic stress disorder, but also with a torn and disrupted understanding of their relationships with God, the world and themselves (cf. ibid., p. 95). The patient may therefore turn his rage and anger also against himself and not only against the abuser (cf. ibid., p. 94). Suicidal thoughts that were put out of question during captivity in order to symbolize resistance may come back and remain long after liberation (cf. ibid., p. 95). Acting out and the repeated reliving of the trauma in the form of flash-backs may be therefore dangerous and threatening. The repetition may have a retraumatizing effect and it can lead to a self-deterioration. This explains the suicide of concentration camp survivors, who felt safe after their survival and committed suicide nevertheless (cf. Caruth 1996, p. 63).

A man-made disaster like the Holocaust causes extreme stress for all victims. The conditions in concentration camps create a surrealistic environment, in which no conventional social structures are present. Additionally to physical degradation, the lack of food, water, warm clothing and socially competent environment, no predictable end to this kind of experience can be set. The victims are thrown into an unacceptable human setting in an unprepared manner (cf. Kahana/Kahana/Zev/Rosner: *Coping with extreme Trauma.* In: *Human Adaptation to Extreme Stress. From the Holocaust to Vietnam.* 1988, pp. 59-61). Extreme traumatic situations like these pose incredible threats to a person´s psyche. Not only does he have to concentrate on survival, but there are also emotional responses to the horrific and dangerous environment he has to deal with. A victim in such a position faces trauma on multiple levels and has many aspects of traumatic encounter while not being able to have periods of temporary relief. He is rather exposed to extreme trauma permanently (cf. ibid., p. 66).

## 2.3 Recovery and the Necessity of a Story

The possession by the victim´s past can never be completely overcome or mastered. A patient is not able to simply go on with the life he had before his trauma and gain complete victory over it (cf. LaCapra 2001, p. 70). A traumatic event is comparable with a foreign body which attacks a person´s very centre of the self (cf. Kapust: *Aussöhnung mit der Fremdheit des Traumas*. In: *Vergessen, vergelten, vergeben, versöhnen? Weiterleben mit dem Trauma*. 2012, p. 107). Trauma can thus be classified as something external and alien. To recover from trauma means finding a way how to live with it, which is still very difficult to accomplish. The acceptance of something alien within ourselves is a very complex and challenging process to go through (cf. ibid., pp. 97-100). The healing of the trauma and of the wound may take an incalculable amount of time for the body as well as for the mind (cf. Fischer 2008, p. 14).

Coping, meaning the favorable reduction of stress (cf. Kahana/Kahana/Harel/Rosner: *Coping with extreme Trauma*. In: *Human Adaptation to Extreme Stress. From the Holocaust to Vietnam*. 1988, p. 56), is often hindered since perceptions of threat in the victim´s environment continue to exist. The survivors feel the need to stay vigilant in the aftermath of trauma. They regard every new situation as threatening and dangerous and the possibility of a life threat is still present (cf. ibid., p. 70). Especially survivors of extreme trauma have difficulties in the aftermath, since certain parallels as vulnerability and dependency, which have now switched from the perpetrators to people in the environment, might bring traumatic memories back (cf. ibid., p. 76).

Recovery is nevertheless possible to some extent when the truth of having lived through a dangerous and horrific event is recognized and acknowledged (cf. Herman 1997, p. 1).

The support from the patient´s environment is very crucial. Immediately after the trauma, the victim needs to rebuild at least a basic form of trust as well as protection and safety. When the feeling of minimal safety is established, the traumatized person has to restore a positive view of himself together with the help of family, friends, partners or the people around him. It is important for this person to be tolerated by others especially when it comes to his oscillation between the desire for closeness and distance at the same time. He also needs to be shown respect for his effort to regain autonomy and self-control (cf. ibid., pp. 61-63).

Although survivors have the willingness to share their traumatic experience with people and long for fairness and compassion, they are often afraid to do so since they do not know how their closest family is going to react: "[...] survivors most often hesitate to disclose to family members, not only because they fear they will not be understood but also because they fear that the reactions of family members will overshadow their own" (ibid., p. 65). Instead of compassion, a survivor is overwhelmed with the other´s reaction to his traumatic past and is not able to cope with his own and other additional responses to it.

The patient needs help from the people that are close to him as well as from the environment in order to mourn the losses that are linked to trauma. There is the necessity of mourning and the support speeds up the healing process. The presence of supportive people has an immense influence on the recovery from trauma. The victim needs recognition and restitution for the resolution of PTSD (cf. ibid., pp. 69-70).

Due to the fact that psychological trauma implies and causes disempowerment and disconnection from others, recovery therefore demands empowerment and reconnection. The healing process is only possible within the framework of relationships. A person cannot achieve success in recovery when he is isolated from others (cf. ibid., p. 133).

Additionally to the support of other people and their advice and affection, the survivor has to be the one in control and he has to be the agent of his empowerment and recovery. He is to be asked about his own wishes and provided as much choice in his actions as possible while still embracing the maintenance of safety (cf. ibid., p. 134).

Prolonged trauma survivors have an excellent intuition for nonverbal and unconscious behavior, which they keep up after the traumatic event: "Accustomed over a long time to reading their captors´ emotional and cognitive states, survivors bring this ability into the therapy relationship" (ibid., p. 139).

Herman suggests three basic stages of recovery, in which she includes the establishment of safety, the reconstruction of the victim´s trauma story and the reconnection between him and the community (cf. ibid., p. 3). She underlines that these stages are an attempt to introduce simplicity and not considered to be a linear straightforward progression that survivors undergo. They may be taken on and given up by victims at any time and all of the sudden. Nevertheless, a change from severe PTSD and dissociation to authentic safety and accepted memory should be visible in the process of recovery (cf. ibid., p. 155). It may occur that patients do not know they suffer from post-traumatic stress disorder. It is particularly important to name the complex trauma and to explain the personality changes it produces to the chronic trauma victims. Since these survivors feel as if they completely lost themselves, they suffer from PTSD extremely and may want to oppose their diagnosis (cf. ibid., pp. 158-159).

At the beginning, it should be the patient´s priority to reestablish a sense of control and power. PTSD victims do not feel secure in their bodies and their thinking. Their sensations are uncontrolled and the relationship to other people is insecure and unsafe. Medicine may help for a short period of time, but the control of the body as well as of the environment must be regained for a long-term successful recovery. This implies getting sleep, eating healthy, doing exercises and developing financial security and a comfortable and sheltered living situation. The victim is able to achieve this aim only with the help of the society (cf. ibid., pp. 159-160). Normal daily activities as shopping, visiting friends or going to work must be possible after establishing safety in body and social contacts. Close family members who decide to participate in creating safety for the victim have to be ready to disrupt their own lives during this time (cf. ibid., p. 162).

A safe environment also demands the designing of a plan for future shelter. The victim himself needs to evaluate the degree of ongoing threat and determine necessary precautions he wants to take (cf. ibid., p. 164). It is crucial for the victim to be the only one in control of the decisions he undergoes (cf. ibid., pp. 166-167). Trauma symptoms may worsen if the step of establishing safety is undervalued. Simply exploring traumatic memories in depth without establishing safety and social support may cause more intrusive symptoms of post-traumatic stress disorder (cf. ibid., pp. 172-173).

The next stage Herman offers is the detailed reconstruction of the trauma story that the victim formulates. The telling itself may be repetitious and emotionless. In this narrative the victim faces his traumatic past and is confronted with the unspeakable. During this act it is still important to keep the feeling of safety balanced against the wish to face the past (cf. ibid., pp. 175-176). The victim´s narrative as a verbal act involves telling another person one´s own past event without merely reciting the facts that are linked to a historical event (cf. Felman: *Camus´ The Plague, or a Monument to Witnessing*. In: *Testimony. Crises of Witnessing in Literature, Psychoanalysis, and History.*1992, p. 93).

The goal is to put the whole story and the trauma into words, together with the emotions the victim feels. What is being created is a verbal, organized and detailed report out of the fragments the victim delivers, which can be put within the framework of time and historical context. Crucial for the creation of the story is the patient´s life before the trauma and the factors that led up to the traumatic event (cf. Herman 1997, pp. 176-177). Gaps and silences during the narrative should be acknowledged and accepted. What needs to be accomplished is the integration of the story into one´s own life (cf. ibid., pp. 180-184). The memories the patient has need to be explored in a careful manner (cf. ibid., p. 184). An important part of the healing process is developing the ability to admit to one´s own emotions (cf. ibid., p. 188). Eventually, after repeated encounters with the memories, the telling of the traumatic event does not arouse the same intense emotions as before and these traumatic memories can be stored as almost "normal" memories (cf. Herman 1997, p. 195).

Although trauma can never be completely forgotten, it can become a part of one´s life that does not control the patient´s mind all the time. As soon as new hope and energy are reconstructed and the past reclaimed, the survivor´s story becomes a past separated from the present and the perspective for future plans is unblocked. The stage of reconstructing a trauma story is accomplished (cf. ibid.).

The therapist takes the role of a listener at all times. There is the necessity of an audience and a listener, though it not necessarily has to be a therapist. It has to be a person who takes on the task of a listener. There is no proper healing process and no telling of a story without an appropriate hearer and response to the trauma narrative (cf. Caruth 1996, p. 9).

The listener becomes a screen, on which the story is projected for the first time. By telling the story the victim hears it for the first time and gets to know the trauma himself. He faces immediate contact with the story and is thus able to witness his own experience anew and get to know it on a different level (cf. Laub: *Bearing Witness, or the Vicissitudes of Listening.* In: Felman/Laub: *Testimony. Crises of Witnessing in Literature, Psychoanalysis, and History.* 1992, p. 57).

Patients often prefer silence, because they shy away from listening to it as well as being listened to (cf. ibid., p. 58). Concentration camps are places of the greatest extent of silence marking a forbidden memory and a black hole, which is so intense that it devours the past. It is too unbearable to speak of it, so there are only unknowable attacks of pain (cf. ibid., p. 64).

Recovery still needs a formulation and an awareness of meaning in the trauma. The patient cannot live his life without having found significance in his experience. This formulation establishes life anew and makes immediate relationships and meaning possible. This can occur when a victim for instance becomes active in a charity or symbolically marks his immortality by having children (cf. Lifton: *Understanding the Traumatized Self. Imagery, Symbolization, and Transformation.* In: *Human Adaptation to Extreme Stress. From the Holocaust to Vietnam.* 1988, p. 26).

The ability to find a formulation for the trauma is a stage, in which the victim finds his meaning. The survivor´s testimony does not have to be historically correct to be valid. The professor Dori Laub deals in his essay *Bearing Witness, or the Vicissitudes of Listening* with the testimony of a woman in the late sixties, who was narrating her Auschwitz experiences to an audience. She reported how she saw four chimneys in the camp explode, when in reality it was only one. Her testimony was considered to be inaccurate. However, it was not the number of chimneys she was truly speaking about, but the unbelievable reality of an unthinkable event (cf. Laub: *Bearing Witness, or the Vicissitudes of Listening.* In: Felman/Laub: *Testimony. Crises of Witnessing in Literature, Psychoanalysis, and History.* 1992, pp. 59-60). The focus lies on the meaning of a narrative itself, as the psychiatrist Judith Greenberg correctly points out. She claims the veracity of traumatic cannot be portrayed completely and whole traumatic artifacts cannot be discovered, so it is impossible to reconstruct true historical facts fully (cf. Greenberg 1998, p. 341).

Not purely documentary information is important for true testimony, but the experience itself underlines the importance of it: "Testimonies are significant in the attempt to understand experience and its aftermath, including the role of memory and its lapses, in coming to terms with – or denying and repressing – the past" (LaCapra 2001, pp. 86-87).

Since the overlapping of true but also forged images in the patient´s memory are consequences of PTSD, the telling of those memories suggests unreliability in the context of "correct" historicity (cf. Evers 2011, p. 16). Facts may not be reported in a correct manner and a degree of unreliability is therefore implied, but what makes testimonies worthy are possible distortions, imaginative transformations and narrative modeling. There is also the potential of repression and denial in those testimonies. The telling implies processes of acting out and a re-experiencing of the traumatic situation. Victims like the woman reporting her Auschwitz experience are acting out by narrating their version of the past, which makes a working through possible at the same time. After repeated descriptions she may eventually come to terms with her past (cf. LaCapra 2011, pp. 88-89).

The reconstruction of a trauma story allows articulation and the transmission of the trauma. A re-externalization takes place. The survivor puts the experience outside of himself and out of his internal system. After that, it is taken inside again with the distance that is required for recovery. The presence of the listener makes that process possible (cf. Laub: *Bearing Witness, or the Vicissitudes of Listening.* In: Felman/Laub: *Testimony. Crises of Witnessing in Literature, Psychoanalysis, and History.* 1992, p. 69). There is also the possibility of an internal witness. A photograph for instance may serve as a substitute for it and the victim may create an artificial witness he narrates his experiences to (cf. Laub: *An Event Without a Witness: Truth, Testimony and Survival.* In: Felman/Laub: *Testimony. Crises of Witnessing in Literature, Psychoanalysis, and History.*1992, pp. 86-87).

Since trauma fragments the victim´s self and possesses him at a later date, the process of telling mirrors the state of PTSD. It mimics the absence of linear and chronological conception that takes place during a traumatic experience. The belated and fragmented return is represented in the narrative. Survivor´s stories lack a beginning, middle, end and are characterized by timelessness. There is no cohesive plot or complete closure (cf. Greenberg 1998, pp. 321-323). The aspect of having survived and the state of having floated between life and death is captured within the narratives as well (cf. ibid, p. 325). As soon as the incomplete fragments are put into a narrative, the signification of the experience is created (cf. ibid., p. 327).

The language of trauma literature and the theory of psychoanalysis both imply the wish for knowing and not knowing about the trauma at the same time (cf. Caruth 1996, p. 3). It visualizes the trauma´s presentable as well as unpresentable clearly in verbal declarations as well as in gaps and silences. The narrative created by a victim, be it oral or written, mimics trauma and implies the lack of integration since trauma negates cognitive integration itself (cf. Rothe 2011, p. 147). Writing and narrating about trauma, including literal aesthetics, can be regarded as a therapeutic procedure, which allows putting trauma into a narrative structure that makes a conscious awareness of it possible (cf. Schmidtgall 2014, p. 112). The integration of trauma into the consciousness succeeds as soon as concealments, gaps and ambiguities are just as much involved as explicit clear statements (cf. ibid., pp. 115-116).

Judith Greenberg claims that: "PTSD might be described as a condition of being possessed by echoes" (cf. Greenberg 1998, p. 326) meaning the voice that tries to tell the victim of the traumatic event which he is not able to grasp yet. There is the possibility of hearing echoes from other people, repeating the victim´s words while giving him the distance he needs for a better understanding of his experience. By hearing his own words aloud, as it is the case in therapy sessions when a therapists repeats the patients words, the echoing of that other person allows the possible recognition of echoes of one´s own talk that otherwise would have remained unrecognized. Echoes, marking an indirect language, can be also found outside of the body, representing telephones, recordings or songs that may tell us of the trauma again. The required distance that is necessary for recovery is given and a recognition of one´s own past made possible. Testimony is crucial for survivors since traumatic stories emerge as fragmentary echoes, beyond any context. With the help of testimony and narration the fragmented echoes can be put into a narrative and trauma can be imbedded (cf. ibid., pp. 330-334).

After the reconstruction of a trauma narrative, Herman speaks of a third category concerning a successful recovery. She advises survivors to undergo a reconnection, in which they create their future and develop a new self as well as new relationships. The victim reclaims his past and develops a new hope and faith for his further journey of life. This step constitutes a difficult progress for victims since coming from an controlled environment, they now face an unfamiliar freedom. The traumatized person continues taking care of his body, his material needs and builds relationships, but performs it more actively now (cf. Herman 1997, pp. 196-197).

In this third step the survivor recognizes he was a victim and comprehends the consequences and facts of his traumatization. He is ready to incorporate his trauma into life and is now clearly aware of the ongoing vulnerability he feels concerning threats. At this point, he is able to actively engage his fear (cf. ibid., p. 197). The level of power and control has increased, so that technically the victim would be ready to react in a dangerous situation as in a fight or battle. He is able to abandon the feeling of shame and guilt and to impose it rightly on the perpetrator (cf. ibid., pp. 199-200).

A basic sense of trust is recreated and the victim developed a new identity now ready to extent his contacts to other people: "As the trauma recedes into the past, it no longer represents a barrier to intimacy" (ibid., p. 206). Intimacy can now evolve. The traumatized victim does not fear the connection to others anymore, especially when it comes to the next generation. In the process of reconnection there is now a possible wish to share the traumatic stories with the children (cf. ibid., pp. 206-207).

A final closure of trauma can never be completed and there may resurface aspects of it during recovery that seemed already completed. The consequences of having experienced a trauma stay with the victim for the rest of his life, but he is able to learn how to live with it to some extent (cf. ibid., p. 211).

# 3.   Trauma in Art Spiegelman's *The Complete Maus*

## 3.1   Reading Comics

The reputation of comics has been associated with poor literacy and restricted intellectual achievements for a long time since comics can be read easily and quickly.

Due to its form, comics were seen as a threat to literacy although its existence can be traced back to the era before film, television or the internet. The acceptance of this medium was thus very hesitant for a long time. In the years between 1967 and 1990 comics began to import literary contents and autobiographies, social protests as well as history were discussed, which increased the general readership. At the beginning of the 1990s, comics became more present in the Western culture (cf. Eisner 2008, pp. xv-xvi).

These days, comics are used in various cultural sectors of life as in entertainment, education, publicity and information. The reading of comics is prevalent in these different areas, which shows that a lot of people make use of the same act of perception. They learn important things about culture by reading comics, as they do for instance with the help of Third World Comics in educational institutions (cf. Silbermann: *The Way Toward a Visual Culture: Comics and Comic Films*. In: *Comics and Visual Culture. Research Studies from ten Countries*. 1986, pp. 22-23).

Comics exist among other things in newspapers, television, books, on packaging, in advertising or on different products sold in stores. Having spread across media, they persist in our world and represent a special mode of communication (cf. Wigand: *Toward a more Visual Culture Through Comics*. In: *Comics and Visual Culture. Research Studies from ten Countries*. 1986, p. 28).

While cartoons can be defined as pictorial representations or caricatures of an idea or a person that as a whole have an influence on the public opinion, comics can be seen as a form of cartooning. They imply a sequence of nearly related drawings whose task it is to educate or entertain (cf. ibid., p. 29).

Will Eisner, one of the most influential comic artists of our times, portrays the basis of storytelling and its usage in comics and graphic novels. By describing images that are put together in a specific order, he speaks of a "sequential art", which defines the specific arrangement of images and texts that together create a story. The storyteller is the person that is in control of the narration. A graphic narrative describes any story that makes use of an image to transmit an idea (cf. Eisner 2008, p. xvii). A story is always told in an ordered and purposeful way (cf. ibid., p. 4). A graphic novel is composed of either a narrative or a dialogue integrated with sequentially depicted art (cf. ibid., p. 140).

The term "graphic novel" is a common and recognizable synonym used for comics worldwide. Since graphic novels took shape as a marketing term, the professor Hillary Chute considers it to be a misnomer and suggests the term "graphic narrative", which regards the problematic issue of a comic being either a work of fiction or non-fiction (cf. Chute 2008, p. 453). The term "graphic narrative" illustrates that historical accuracy is not contrary to creative invention and fiction (cf. ibid., p. 459).

A graphic storytelling implies an emotional charge that is transmitted to the reader: "There is a psychic transmission present in the best storytelling. It is generated by the storyteller´s passion. It carries the story´s emotional charge to the reader" (Eisner, p. 153). Feelings, emotions and values are communicated through the artwork to the reader. The storyteller identifies himself to some extent with the narrative and becomes a part of it (cf. ibid.).

Comics consist of juxtaposed and spatially adjacent pictures (cf. McCloud 1994, p. 7) that are drawn within frames called "panels" and contain text, dialogues or onomatopoeias in speech balloons or spaces for captions. Text and images are separate signs, but refer to each other and are thus linked. Comics are self-referential. Words refer to images and vice versa. As soon as text and image are read together, the meaning of the message is produced. There is no such thing as an universal truth, since the combination of text and images can produce versions of truth depending on the reader´s own ability to create meaning. The repetition of an image, figure or word shown in a panel before does not have the exact same meaning in a different panel. The identical depiction does not necessarily bear the same meaning in a different position of the comic (cf. ibid., p. 327).

The comic´s special feature is the provided imagery. The arrangement of text and imagery influences the quality of the story telling, in which the reader is called to actively participate. The reader works through the comic at his own pace providing sound and action internally that support the images (cf. Eisner 2008, p. 69).

Not only does he read abstract icons that show no resemblance to real objects or persons, which enlarges his imagination (cf. McCloud 1994, p. 29), but he also reads and creates the message in what is not shown in the comic. The reader is encouraged to give life to the story he reads by undergoing the procedure of what McCloud calls "closure". It is a: "[…] phenomenon of observing the parts but perceiving the whole […]" (ibid., p. 63). We perform closure every day by completing in our minds what is incomplete based on our past experience. We know, for instance, that we have to take money from our pockets when we want to buy a product at the checkout counter. In comics, the reader is therefore a collaborator, who consciously and by choice commits closure between the panels, which McCloud calls "the gutter". That is the place where the imagination works by combining separate images and transforming them into a complete idea. The experience tells the reader that something must be in the gutter, although there is no image depicted there (cf. ibid., pp. 63-66).

The reading of a comic is dependent on the reader´s cultural knowledge. The abstract and symbolic representation of reality in comics offers a broad projection area for the reader. He is the one who fills this area with his own cultural meaning patterns (cf. Schmidtgall 2014, p. 127)

Comic panels offer a ragged sense of disconnected moments. Closure makes the connection of those moments possible and a unified and continuous reality may resurface (cf. McCloud 1994, p. 67). By performing the continuous act of closure, time and motion are simulated and a narrative develops (cf. ibid., p. 69).

Words create a sense of time by depicting sounds. The bigger the lettering in comics, the louder is the sound level figuratively (cf. Eisner 2008, p. 61). There is also the possibility of a linking between space and time. The bigger the space, the bigger the time frame (cf. McCloud 1994, p. 101). Borderless panels may portray timelessness, because they go beyond any restricted frames (cf. ibid., p. 102). Shape therefore goes hand in hand with temporal duration.

Although comics are primarily a visual and mono-sensory medium, in the gutter none of our senses are needed. This means that all of our senses are engaged during that time. The reader is practically invited to read the visible as well as the invisible and not only see what is shown, but also what is not shown (cf. ibid., pp. 89-93).

The emotions that are transmitted are central to graphic narratives. Colors may also cause certain sensations in the reader. It is crucial for a communication to consider the colors or the lack of color in a comic. The latter may have a more direct communication in mind (cf. ibid., pp. 190-192).

Comics are a medium of communication. The artist brings to paper what he has in mind. His idea wanders from the paper to the eye and the mind of the audience and this way the message is communicated. The dialogue is only effective when the reader comprehends the special forms that this medium demonstrates. That is why for a successful transmission of the storyteller´s message it is relevant for readers of comics to understand how to properly read them (cf. ibid., pp. 194-198).

## 3.2 Direct and Indirect Trauma

Art Spiegelman published his work in two volumes in 1986 and 1991 respectively (cf. Doherty 1996, p. 70). *The Complete Maus* includes part I entitled "A Survivor's Tale: My father bleeds history" and part II "And here my troubles began". *The Complete Maus* still maintains this division and in 1992 Spiegelman won the Pulitzer Prize for his work. In his comic narrative he portrays the topic of the Holocaust in an unconventional way and permits the intersection of art and history (cf. Zeitlin 1998, p. 6).

Spiegelman's work of art is a depiction of Holocaust survivors and their experiences as well as the transmission of those from father to son (cf. Mc Glothlin 2008, p. 99). The son of the Auschwitz survivor Vladek Spiegelman, who survives World War II and eventually emigrates to America, talks about his father's experiences and describes his traumatic past during the war as well as after it. He records his father's narration, writes it down and simultaneously searches for the effects and the impact these recollections have on his father's and his own lives (cf. Banner 2000, p. 5). Additionally, Art, the implied author, depicts his own feelings he has concerning his parent's lives and their past.

The comic narrative goes back and forth in time. It goes from New York, where both father and son have their conversations, and Poland, where Vladek's narrative is based upon. Past and present alternate and there are two levels of narrative time. On the one hand there is the wartime narrative of 1930's/1940's and on the other hand there is the reconstruction of the story that takes place in 1970's/1980's (cf. Elmwood 2004, p. 695).

Spiegelman draws different people and races by using the images of animals. He draws the Jews as mice who are chased by the Germans depicted as cats. The Poles are portrayed as pigs and Americans as dogs, who according to the natural food chain chase the cats. Art´s father Vladek is presented as a young, ambitious man before and during the war. Due to his wily character and his talent for skilled labor, he manages to survive the war and the time in the concentration camp in Auschwitz. After the war Vladek´s character changes drastically. He is frail, runs out of breath easily and lacks the independence and determination he used to have during the war. After Auschwitz, he suffers from posttraumatic stress disorder, which accumulates first of all due to the traumatic past under occupation.

Vladek´s son Art asks his father to tell him about the past, his life in Poland and the war based on his wish to draw a book about that topic. Vladek´s reaction to it is contradictory. On the one hand he claims that no one would want to hear these stories and that merely one book would not suffice for all his experiences. On the other hand he begins to tell his story anyway saying: "BUT, IF YOU WANT, I CAN TELL YOU…" (Spiegelman 2003, p. 14). According to Herman, the will to keep the past a secret and the desire to proclaim it go hand in hand in trauma theory. This exact behavior can be seen in Vladek´s statement. He does not want to go back to the traumatic past, yet he wants to be heard eventually and takes the risk to declare it.

Vladek is possessed by PTSD at a later date. The topic of the war occupies his mind several years after it. By the time his son Art, who was born after the war, is already an adult, Vladek goes back in time and tells him the story of his traumatic past. Art visits his father regularly and asks him to tell him more about the war every time, so Vladek repeatedly returns to this topic (cf. ibid., p. 45). Vladek, being a typical trauma victim, returns repeatedly to his trauma with a delayed response.

He experiences a lot of loss during the war as well as after it. He loses most of his family members including his father, siblings, nephews and nieces as well as his little son Richieu during the war. From his entire family only the little brother survives (cf. ibid., p. 276). He loses a feeling of security as well as of safety and home due to his persecution.

Since Vladek survives and most of his and his wife´s family does not (cf. ibid.), he experiences survivor guilt, which is verbally suggested by a therapist that the son visits a long time after Vladek´s death: "Maybe your father needed to show that he was always right – that he could always SURVIVE – because he felt GUILTY about surviving" (ibid., p. 204). Vladek expresses this guilt by undermining Art´s abilities. At some point, Vladek accidently tips over the pills he has been counting and putting into order and accuses Art of distracting him. He blames Art for his own mistake: "ALWAYS WE PUSHED YOUR ARM DOWN; AND YOU WOULD **OOPS!** LOOK NOW WHAT YOU MADE ME DO!" (ibid., p. 32). When Art offers re-counting them for him, Vladek replies: "**NO!** YOU DON´T KNOW COUTNING PILLS: I´LL DO IT AFTER…I´M AN **EXPERT** FOR THIS" (ibid.). He gives Art the feeling of not being able to do simple things as counting pills. Vladek compensates his guilt by proving to himself that he has special abilities no one else has, which even possibly helped him to survive. He disguises the inferiority and guilt that he feels towards the dead by putting himself on a pedestal and Art somewhere below.

The counting of pills as well as nail sorting (cf. ibid., p. 100), the counting of crackers (cf. ibid., p. 237) and the fondness for fixing broken things in the house he expresses again and again (cf. ibid., p. 277) can be categorized as repetition compulsion. Vladek himself claims: "IT´S **ALWAYS** SOMETHING HERE I MUST DO" (ibid., p. 100). He does these daily tasks with determination, which is typical of trauma survivors. He returns repeatedly to an act that guarantees him a sense of control. Since he lost that control, he turns to the counting that gives him order and regularity, which is clearly emphasized in a sequence when Vladek articulates the counting aloud: "..11…12…13.. I´M MAKING INTO

DAILY PORTIONS MY PILLS....14...15.." (ibid., p. 28). The reliance on this order gives him the stability that his trauma experience took from him.

Not only does he need the assurance for a controlled daily run, but he is also concerned with controlling people around him. He is commanding and dominant with his own family members. He throws Art´s coat out without Art´s permission and replaces it with a new one that eventually turns out to be too big for his son. He behaves in a controlling and imperative way and does not react to Art´s objection to it at all (cf. ibid., pp. 70-71). Vladek brings a sense of control back into his life by retaining control in every aspect concerning his or his family member´s lives.

The persecution of Jews and the captivity in the concentration camp in Auschwitz, which can be categorized as prolonged or complex trauma, depicts an ongoing tense situation from the beginning until the end of the war. It started as soon as Vladek went to the frontier to fight against Germany (cf. ibid., p. 40). He and his family did not have any temporal relief during this time.

Especially after prolonged trauma victims have health issues. Vladek also suffers from hemorrhaging, glaucoma (cf. ibid., p. 41), diabetes and a heart disease (cf. ibid., p. 28), which may as well be due to his older age, but is also connected to bodily aches that come into being after experiencing trauma. Vladek talks about his state as if he was still in captivity: "FOR MY CONDITION I MUST FIGHT TO *SAVE* MYSELF" (ibid.). The emphasis is put on the survival and the reader associates it immediately with the Holocaust and his concentration camp experience.

There are several moments, in which Vladek relives the past and is acting it out. Vladek collects and saves little things that could come in handy and that could be useful. He saves a plastic pitcher from a hospital room that is a year old (cf. ibid., p. 95) and picks up telephone wires, which according to Vladek are difficult to find (cf. ibid., p. 118). Those things were not available during the war.

Vladek tells Art that **"ALWAYS** I SAVED…JUST IN CASE!"** (ibid., p. 65) during the war. He behaves the same way now that the war is over and confuses the present with the past. He fears a repetition of these situations he experienced, when it was difficult to find or purchase things. He saves useful objects now just in case it happens again. The link between past and present can be seen even in Vladek´s narrative. He speaks in present tense while describing a situation in which he tried to get away from the Germans in 1941: "WILL I WALK **SLOWLY**, THEY WILL TAKE ME…WILL I RUN THEY CAN SHOOT ME!"(ibid. p. 82) Vladek talks as if he was still in this situation and is thrown back into the past. He does not separate past and present and relives this moment again. The acting out does not allow any distance from this past situation.

Vladek tries to convince his son several times to quit smoking (cf. ibid., p. 180), which not only occurs due to his concern about Art´s health, but also because in Auschwitz one could have exchanged cigarettes for bread (cf. ibid., 224). It was beneficial to not smoke and Vladek considers it to be beneficial now as well, in case of repeated captivity. This is emphasized by the repetitive use of present tense by Vladek, in which he confuses the past and the present again. Even in the very last sequence Vladek confuses Art with his late son Richieu, who died during the war, which according to Elmwood reveals how present Richieu still is to the father (cf. Elmwood 2004, p. 704).

Being in the state of hyperarousal and anticipating a possible return of traumatic events goes hand in hand with Vladek´s aggressive behavior. He expresses a deep anger and has outbursts of fury to strangers as well as family members. Not only does he talks aggressively with Art when he tips over the pills or when Art arrives late (cf. Spiegelman 2003, p. 75), but he also reacts this way to Art´s wife Francoise when they are going by car to exchange groceries. She stops driving in order to talk to a hitch-hiker. Vladek gets furious and starts protesting loudly, which can be in seen in the bold type used here: **"HAH?! WHAT FOR**

**DO YOU STOP, FRANCOISE? WE´RE NOT YET TO THE BUNGA-LOW?"** (ibid., p. 258). As soon as Vladek recognizes that the hitch-hiker is a Black man, he tells Francoise even louder to: **"PUSH QUICK ON THE GAS!"** (ibid.). Vladek expresses his worry that the Black man could steal the groceries he has bought earlier. He regards the Black man to be less worthy and copies the racist behavior he learned during the war. He is controlled by the rules of captivity and the norm of the Holocaust. Auschwitz is still present in his mind, where racial segregation, prejudice and the existence of subhuman beings were exemplified. Vladek may also mentally apply the role of an enemy here, who could worsen Vladek´s "status" if he would be seen with a "[…] A **SHVARTZER!"** (ibid.) by someone else. Since Vladek had rapport with guards and block supervisors due to his special language abilities (cf. ibid., p. 195), one could imagine that he would not want to ruin this advantage by being seen with a man who would be regarded as inferior and subhuman in Holocaust norms. This man is an enemy who could harm him. It could be unprofitable to know him. This mirrors another form of acting out, in which Vladek is constantly vigilant and confusing the present with the past. Spiegelman himself considers Vladek´s racism in this sequence to be a consequence of the Holocaust and part of his difficult character (cf. Spiegelman 2011, p. 36). Vladek´s personality before the war was caring, soft and kind (cf. Spiegelman 2003, p. 125) and after it he changed into an intolerant and impatient survivor (cf. ibid., p. 179).

Vladek´s racial attitude also reveals how disconnected he is from society and his closest environment. He does neither trust in a safe environment nor in comfort or shelter. His sense of security is demolished. He is isolated and feels alone. At one point, he runs from the hospital he stayed in, because he does not trust the doctors there (cf. ibid., p. 281).

Towards the end of the graphic narrative, Art and Vladek look at family pictures. They depict members of Anja´s family who died during the war (cf. ibid.,

p. 275). According to Spiegelman himself, the pile of photos resemble a pile of bodies and show the loss the family had to experience (cf. Spiegelman 2011, p. 222). Shortly after this sequence, Vladek is sitting on a couch and is depicted in several panels that form one big image (cf. Spiegelman 2003, p. 276). Spiegelman emphasizes his loneliness, isolation and disconnection from the world (cf. Spiegelman 2011, p. 232).

Vladek also portrays his helplessness and loneliness and underlines his victimhood. When Art refuses to help him in the house, Vladek organizes someone else to do that. However, he points out that: "[…] AT LEAST **SOMEBODY** WILL HELP ME!" (Spiegelman 2003, p. 99).

Since, according to Herman, trauma destroys one´s self-perception, Vladek as a trauma victim is disconnected from himself, but does not see that. It is almost impossible to make him happy, as Art points out (cf. ibid., p. 172), but Vladek himself does not see that. The reason for Vladek´s isolation and loneliness is partly because nobody is able to please him. Since he does not tolerate any mistakes and: "[…] straightens everything you touch […]" (ibid., p. 182), he withdraws from relationships and sticks to isolation. Nevertheless, he longs for closeness and intimacy. This oscillation is typical of trauma survivors. They step back from closeness, but have a strong desire for it at the same time. Vladek pushes people away, but tries to convince Art and Francoise to stay for the whole summer with him at the Catskills (cf. ibid., p. 177). He does not seem to accept Art´s statement that they are going to stay there for just a few days. Shortly after Art´s refusal, he again insists they stay longer: "MAYBE WE´LL **TOGETHER** STAY TO THE END OF THE SUMMER HERE…" (ibid., p. 184).

There is very little intimacy between Vladek, Art and his second wife Mala, whom Vladek talks down to and does not seem to appreciate (cf. ibid., p. 229). Mala, who tries to please him, but does not achieve it, accuses Vladek to be

"[…] MORE ATTACHED TO THINGS THAN PEOPLE!" (ibid., p. 95). This behavior is also typical of trauma survivors and first generation members.

The tattooed number on Vladek´s arm, a permanent scar on his body, is a continuous reminder of the past (cf. ibid., p. 252). Although the body is affected beyond doubt, Banner highlights the hopelessness of mental escape from Auschwitz. Vladek talks about his arrival to Auschwitz and tells his son how: "[…] WE KNEW THAT FROM HERE WE WILL NOT COME OUT ANYMORE…" (ibid., p. 159). Vladek survived physically, but his captivity still continues mentally (cf. Banner 2000, p. 169).

Vladek suffers from insomnia (cf. Spiegelman 2003, p. 177). When he is already asleep, he has nightmares, which become audible through groans and moaning (cf. ibid., p. 234). This shows that Vladek, not only suffers from hyperarousal, but also from intrusion, one of Herman´s categories of PTSD. It includes reliving trauma through nightmares and flashbacks. According to Banner, the sound that Vladek makes in his sleep (cf. ibid.) and the sound that a prisoner in Auschwitz makes also during sleeping (cf. ibid., p. 219), resemble highly (cf. Banner 2000, p. 168). The reader immediately thinks that Vladek must be dreaming about his Auschwitz experience. His traumatic past haunts him in his sleep and he relives it in his nightmares.

The statement which introduces the reader to the second chapter of the second part of Spiegelman´s work "Auschwitz (Time Flies)" indicates the lack of a narrative chronology as well (cf. Mandaville 2009, p. 222) and the delayed response that Auschwitz has 70 years after its occurrence. McGlothin connects this statement to the nature of trauma emphasizing its persistent nature and static, but continuous timelessness (cf. McGlothlin: *"When time stands still": Traumatic Immediacy and Narrative Organization in Art Spiegelman´s Maus and In the Shadow of No Towers.* In: *The Jewish Graphic Novel. Critical Approaches.* 2008, p. 105).

In addition to the trauma of Vladek´s Auschwitz and war experience, another incident contributes to his PTSD. His wife Anja commits suicide many years after the war without leaving a note. Art is already older at that point. Vladek states how, years after this incident, he still thinks about her every day (cf. ibid., p. 263). He is not able to accept the loss: "EVERYWHERE I LOOK I´M SEEING ANJA…" (ibid., p. 263).

At some point, Vladek tells Art about some diaries that his mother Anja wrote. Art desperately wants to find them to see what his mother wrote about her past and her experiences. Not until much later does he find out that Vladek destroyed and burned her notebooks: "ONE TIME I HAD A VERY BAD DAY…AND ALL OF THESE THINGS I **DESTROYED**" (ibid., p. 160). They worked as a flashback to Vladek and reminded him painfully of the past. As Banner points out, Vladek destroys Anja´s journals to escape the hurtful memories of the past (cf. Banner 2000, p. 153). He flees from reality. After learning this, Art gets furious and calls his father a: "…MURDERER" (Spiegelman 2003, p. 161). Vladek is not able to cope with the past and as a form of acting out, eliminates his wife and her remains on purpose. Every now and then though, his attachment to Anja prevails while his second wife Mala feels underappreciated and cannot compete with Anja: "YOUR FATHER! HE TREATS ME AS IF I WERE A MAID OR HIS NURSE […]" (ibid., p. 132).

Vladek also throws letters away that a French co-prisoner sent him (cf. ibid., p. 258). At first, he saved them, but eventually he threw them away together with Anja´s notebooks (cf. ibid., p. 258). By doing this, Vladek blocks the past since he is unable to cope with it. He tries to eliminate it from consciousness and his unwillingness to accept the loss keeps him in the state of melancholia.

Anja is depicted as a very frail woman, who was hysterical and depressed before the war and after her little son´s birth (cf. ibid., p. 33). Unlike Vladek, she is a passive figure, who does not handle the dangerous situations she is in as good as her husband. The category of PTSD that is to be ascribed in Anja's situation is the state of constriction, even if it is a delayed state, because she surrenders to her trauma and, as a sign of indifference, kills herself several years after the war. The last talk that Art has with her is very short and discomforting. Anja looks for a conversation with her son, but does not get any response from him. He ignores her need for comfort (cf. ibid., p. 105). Since she does not get a proper response nor comfort from her environment, no healing of her mental state can occur and she gives in. She does not reconnect, but lingers in her loneliness. The mental state that bothers her may very likely derive from the war experiences in Auschwitz, the treatments she got there (cf. ibid., p. 213) and losses she sustained. We learn that her nephew was sent to Auschwitz, that she lost her family and refused to live: "LET ME ALONE! I DON'T WANT TO LIVE!" (ibid., p. 124). After the war, Anja's brother dies from a hit-and-run driver in 1964, which, according to Vladek, made Anja die a little as well (cf. ibid., p. 274).

The situations that cause Anja's trauma are merely speculations since the reader never gets to see her version of the story. Vladek is the one talking about Anja and her past. Elmwood emphasizes that Anja is portrayed through Vladek's eyes throughout the whole narrative (cf. Elmwood 2004, p. 691). We find out more about Vladek than about his wife by the way he describes her. Her consciousness or perspective is not available in the whole comic narrative (cf. ibid., p. 712).

Art experiences traumata on different levels. As Hirsch precisely explains, the trauma of Anja's suicide activates the trauma of his parents' past (cf. Hirsch 2012, p. 43). He feels guilty, because he did not react to her need to talk and connect with him. He is directly traumatized by her suicide, but not directly by her past, since he is not able to neither talk to her about her past nor see her journals.

Art articulates his trauma in a comic entitled "Prisoner On The Hell Planet", which Vladek eventually reads and which reminds him of Anja's loss. As a flashback and reminder of the trauma of his wife's suicide, Vladek suffers from it to the extent that he is not able to work it through yet. By blocking it and trying to eliminate it from consciousness, he puts his feelings and emotions concerning her loss far.

Art, traumatized by the suicide, expresses his numbness, confusion and guilt in his comic distributed on four pages (cf. Spiegelman 2003, pp. 102-105). He cannot forgive himself for not helping her and not hearing her out: "THE GUILT WAS OVERWHELMING!" (ibid., p. 104). The unspeakability of Art's trauma during the incident is noticeable in the fact that he articulates it four year after this incident. It possesses him at a later date. He draws himself in a prisoner uniform and represents himself crying in a closed cell. This portrays his isolation from the outside world.

Art, experiencing a direct trauma, is also vicariously traumatized by the Holocaust experiences he hears. According to William, new trauma accumulates more easily, so Art is very sensitive after his mother's suicide to his parents' past his father tells him.

Laub claims that listeners to other people's trauma are likely to feel confusion, dread or bewilderment and witness not only emotions in the survivors, but also within themselves. Art is able to put his emotions concerning Anja's suicide onto paper and publishes the comic. Elmwood argues that although both traumata are linked and Art suffers from direct trauma, because Anja killed herself because of her direct trauma, Art manages to keep his direct and indirect trauma separated (cf. Elmwood 2004, p. 703). His short comic strip allows him to put the trauma into words and into a narrative that points to a resolution (cf. Elmwood 2004, p. 711). A narration of his traumatic experience allows a working through.

By hearing Vladek´s stories and by hearing the tape recorder, to which he repeatedly turns and which acts as an repetitive echo of the traumatic past, Art vicariously suffers from PTSD. By hearing his father´s trauma there is an encounter with Art´s own trauma, which helps him to get in touch with his own feelings, so he can start working through.

Art is able to reveal and expose his emotions concerning his mother´s suicide. For a successful coping with a traumatic past, a narration that includes emotions and integrates them in a story is necessary. Art manages to do that in his comic strip and the reader is not reminded of Art´s numbness or anger for Anja anymore. Vladek does not expose his emotions in his narrative. He presents his memory, but he does that emotionless. He does not reveal enough emotions neither while narrating nor does the reader get access to the emotions Vladek feels during his traumatic situations.

Banner claims that Art is very reminiscent of a therapist, who takes notes and tapes the patient. He reminds Vladek every time where he stopped his story and does not interrupt his father during his narration. After their meeting they part and meet again for the next "session" (cf. Banner 2000, p. 138). Eventually, Vladek tells and creates a coherent story for himself. He also inscribes himself onto Art´s paper and draws a bunker that he built during the war (cf. Spiegelman 2003, p. 112). He communicates himself and actively participates in Art´s creation. Partially, he makes the connection to the outside world.

Art is someone that represents an audience and a listener, which is necessary for recovery. For a complete successful healing however Vladek´s missing emotions in his story are inevitable. The "Prisoner on the Hell Planet" includes the emotions Art felt during and after the traumatic event of Anja´s suicide (cf. Spiegelman 2011, p. 149). Since it was published, it can be read by an audience and receives a proper response.

## 3.3 The Parallelism between Graphic Narrative and Trauma

Hillary Chute argues that Art Spiegelman´s comic is extremely complex in an aesthetic and political sense, which is specific to this medium. She considers this work of art to be an absorbing story, which portrays history combined with torture and massacre, which does not turn away from trauma, but with the help of a visual backtracking opens up to it and deals with it (cf. Chute 2008, pp. 456-459).

The graphic narrative presents many possibilities of depicting trauma, as has been shown in the previous chapter. There are several panels that demonstrate traumatization, as for instance the panel that presents the arrival to Auschwitz. It is by far the biggest in the entire comic. It is also drawn without borders (cf. Spiegelman 2003, p. 159), which in a comic signifies the importance of timelessness. According to Laub, trauma lacks a beginning, middle or end and is therefore characterized by timelessness. The moment of the arrival in Auschwitz represents the starting point of Vladek´s trauma.

Schmidtgall turns to the form of the graphic narrative. By comparing it to the experience of trauma he discovers commonalities between the comic and the condition of PTSD. He claims that the form of the comic acts as a counterpart of the nature of trauma, which is characterized by its unspeakability and the desire to proclaim it. The presentable and describable in trauma is recognizable within the depicted panels. The gutter between the panels marks the unpresentable of the trauma. The alternation of the gutter and the panels helps to break down this contrary structure (cf. Schmidtgall 2014, p. 126).

What is not presentable is nevertheless portrayed and the readers constructs the whole picture of the trauma by performing closure. He puts the pieces of the panels and the gutter together and creates a coherent story of the traumatic past the victim experienced. At the same time, this structure does not overburden the reader or the author himself. It makes a construction of a narrative space possible, which enables the rehabilitation of the trauma without direct images (cf. ibid.).

The form of the graphic narrative with its historical content generates the process of sense making, which is created with the help of its images, texts and symbols as well as closure. The subjective experience of closure while reading and the lack of an objective truth at the same time enable the finding of a meaning by the reader himself (cf. ibid.).

There is also the use of wordless panels in the comic narrative (cf. Spiegelman 2003, p. 205). One may assume that it demonstrates the inability to find language and words that is typical of the condition of PTSD.

The distance from a traumatic situation that is needed for a successful recovery is recognizable within the comic form as well. The lacking interspace between some of the panels mirror the missing distance from the past traumatic event. When Art and Vladek have one of their conversations, they are separated by a panel that depicts the past (cf. ibid., 137). This panel is depicted with borders, it nevertheless touches father and son respectively without leaving a blank space. The same occurs with the huge panel showing the arrival to Auschwitz. It does not leave any blank spaces between the upper panels and no distance can be observed here.

McGlothlin suggests that the lack of color in the graphic novel foregrounds distance and maintains it (cf. McGlothlin: *"When time stands still": Traumatic Immediacy and Narrative Organization in Art Spiegelman´s Maus and In the Shadow of No Towers. In: The Jewish Graphic Novel. Critical Approaches.* 2008 p. 99). The black and white is also reminiscent of photographies that were taken back then, which also lack color. The link to the past is made also with the help of this device.

Art´s comic strip "Prisoner on the Hell Planet", which is incorporated in *The Complete Maus*, represents Art´s own direct trauma that is distinctive from

Vladek´s trauma depicted in the bigger graphic narrative. The son´s trauma deals with his mother´s suicide and Vladek´s trauma mainly with the Holocaust. The "Prisoner on the Hell Planet", which stands out visually from the rest (cf. Elmwood 2004, p. 711), is thus a comic within a bigger comic. Since both generations have to deal with their traumata, it also signifies a trauma within a trauma. Art is traumatized by the huge topic of the Holocaust, which has been activated by his mother´s suicide. The suicide plays a certain part within his indirect vicarious trauma concerning the parents´ past. Anja kills herself due to her past experiences and traumatization during the war, as one might assume, and this suicide causes Art´s direct trauma. As Hirsch states, the trauma of Anja´s suicide activates the transposition to the parents´ trauma (cf. Hirsch 2012, p. 43).

The short comic strip and its integration within the bigger comic narrative mirrors this fact. The direct trauma of his mother´s suicide is integrated within the indirect trauma that he experiences later on as an adult.

# 4. The Concept of Postmemory

## 4.1 Familial Transmission of Trauma

The consequences of a man-made disaster like the Holocaust are not only experienced by people who survived it or had direct contact with it, but also by the victims´ children, who are emotionally as well as socially affected (cf. Kahana/Harel/Kahana: *Predictors of Psychological Well-Being among Survivors of the Holocaust*. In: *Human Adaptation to Extreme Stress. From the Holocaust to Vietnam*. 1988, p. 172). The following generations seem to be preoccupied more and more with the Shoah many years after it took place. They are now ready to travel back in time in order to contemplate it from a temporal distance and explore the ways it affects their own lives (cf. Hoffman 2004, p. ix). The term "survivor´s child" is assigned to those who were born after their parents had been liberated and who did not witness persecution themselves (cf. Kestenberg/ Kestenberg: *The Background of the Study*. In: *Generations of the Holocaust*. 1988, p. 42).

There is no homogenous rule that can be applied to the transmission of traumata, because not all survivors behave in the same manner towards their children. Just like every patient reacts differently to a traumatic situation, the transmission of it may differ as well. Some victims transmit their trauma by simply continuing to live in the shadow of the past. Other parents compare their offspring to the dead children they lost during the Holocaust. By doing this, they force them to live two lives at the same time meaning the present life as well as the past one that included the dead loved child. Yet others put their children on a level with the persecutor (cf. Bergmann/Jucovy: *Epilogue*. In: *Generations of the Holocaust*. 1988, p. 311). The different ways in which parents react towards their children and transmit their traumatic experiences will be presented in detail shortly.

First, a definition of the term "postmemory" will be given in order to allow a better understanding of the transmission of trauma from parents to children. Marianne Hirsch, a professor of English and Comparative Literature, describes postmemory as a "[…] relationship that the "generation after" bears to the personal, collective, and cultural trauma of those who came before – to experiences they "remember" only by means of the stories, images, and behaviors among which they grew up" (Hirsch 2012, p. 5). Those images and stories were transferred intensively and powerfully, so that children of survivors may consider the parents´ memories to be their own. However, they are not their own real memories and there are no true recalls from the past. The link to this past they have never lived through is nevertheless made by imaginative investment as well as creation and projection (cf. ibid.). The children engage themselves in the parents´ or ancestors´ lives before or during the war and involve themselves in the past lives with the help of imaginative participation.

There is a certain danger involved when hearing stories and growing up with memories that are not one´s own and that took place before one´s birth. The own life story takes the risk to be displaced or even relinquished by the stories of the parents or forefathers. The life of the survivors´ child is sculptured by traumatic fragmented pieces of events or situations that are still not fully or easily comprehended (cf. ibid.).

The structure of postmemory is formed by the link between an event in the past and its impact in the present. The "post" in the term "postmemory" means more than just a temporal postponement or a place in the aftermath. It portrays more than a successive temporality or logic. Hirsch takes into consideration other "posts" that concern different intellectual territories stating how "postmodernism and "poststructuralism" determine a distance as well as interrelation with and interdependence between modernism and structuralism. "Postcolonial", for instance, does not signify the end of the colonial, but a complex continuity instead, while "postfeminist" depicts the succession of feminism. Hirsch states that we still find ourselves in the era of "posts", which seems to increase as can be seen in terms as "posttraumatic", "posthuman" or "postracial". The various layers as well as the belatedness included in these different "posts" is implied also in postmemory (cf. ibid.). It mirrors a restless oscillation between rupture and continuity. It depicts not an actual movement, but rather "[…] a *structure* of inter- and intragenerational return of traumatic knowledge and embodied experience" (ibid., p. 6).

Postmemory and memory are not identical, but they match regarding the affective power and psychic consequences they both entail (cf. ibid., p. 31). Memory depicts an affective linking to the past and a sense of a material connection, which is conveyed by literature, films, photography and testimonies (cf. ibid., p. 33). The memory transmitted to the descendants, sometimes across three to even four generations, is accompanied by the wish to institutionalize this memory in archives, books, commemorations or rituals. Postmemory is composed of a continuity that expresses itself across generations. It also mirrors the various ruptures and gaps imposed by trauma and depicts how they affect intra-, inter- as well as transgenerational legacy. There are ruptures involved caused by collective historical trauma as erasures of records, missing possessions and denied histories under the Nazi regime. Postmemory works against those losses and tries to reactivate political and cultural memorial procedures by creating individual and familial forms of mediation and aesthetic ideas (cf. ibid. pp. 32-33). Memory culture keeps growing due to a possible need for an individual as well as group inclusion in a collectivity fabricated by a common inheritance of various traumatic stories. Another factor for the growing need may be the social and individual responsibility the descendants feel towards an inherited and ongoing traumatic past (cf. ibid., pp. 33-34).

The transmission of trauma takes place most likely in a familial space. The language of the body within this space is represented by precognitive and nonverbal acts of transfer, which frequently take the shape of symptoms (cf. ibid., p. 34).

Nonverbal behavior may involve movements that have a specific intention of sending a message to a listener. The person has the ability to choose between expressing a message with his face or his body. These movements are often used when the speaker could actually speak but chooses not to. A person may, for instance, shrug his shoulders while saying the words "I do not know" (cf. Ehman: *Three Classes of Nonverbal Behavior.* In: *Aspects of Nonverbal Communication*, 1980. p. 90). Information can also be transmitted via behavior without the speaker´s knowing of it. Blushing, eye positioning or hand and head movements often express information unintentionally. Verbal and nonverbal behaviors may also give very contradictory information (cf. White : *Nonverbal Antecedents to Language Functioning: A Model and its Relevance for the Deaf.* In: *Nonverbal Communication Today. Current Research.* 1982, p. 233).

Postmemory does not portray an identity status, but a generational structure or composition of transmission that can be mediated in various ways. The family´s life is ingrained in a collective imaginary that is formed by public organizations of projection and by a shared archive of narratives and images that influence the availability of individual and familial recollection. There are two groups that are affected by the remembrance of the past. There is on the one hand a group of people, who lived in survivor families and grew up with their stories, so that identification, projection as well as imagination might have taken place very likely. On the other hand there is a group of people less proximate to the survivors´ immediate past. They are characterized by curiosity and an urge to know about the past, but they did not have direct contact with the victim´s traumatic experiences (cf. Hirsch 2012, p. 35). Hirsch speaks of "familial" and "affiliative" postmemory characterizing the former as an intergenerational structure taking place between child and parent and the latter as an intragenerational formation, which can be identified as a loosened version of the previous structure. In affiliative postmemory the child is more broadly receptive to other contemporary ways of mediation (cf. ibid., p. 36). In the structure of familial postmemory children are mostly affected by parental transmission, which will be examined in more detail shortly.

In After such Knowledge, the writer and professor Eva Hoffman reveals her own life story as a child of survivors and incorporates her own experiences as well as conversations with other descendants of Holocaust victims in her work. She emphasizes the invasion of the war into the structure of her childhood from the very beginning. The knowledge she received from her parents was the first knowledge of her life. On the basis of the knowledge of a horrific past, which was deeply internalized and weirdly unknown, grew everything else and every other knowledge (cf. Hoffman 2004, pp. 3-6). Those memories were not primarily expressed by the victims themselves, but it was rather: "[…] something more potent and less lucid; something closer to enactment of experience, to emanations or sometimes nearly embodiments of psychic matter […] (ibid., p. 7).

In the language of the family transmission takes place more directly and more ruthless than in public or social speeches. Dialogues with intimates, spouses and children allow a chaos of emotions and the lack of coherent stories that survivors tend to communicate (cf. ibid., p. 9). The emanations of the parents´ tormented past that the children received: "[…] kept erupting in flashes of imagery; in abrupt, fragmented phrases; in repetitions, broken refrains" (ibid., p. 9). Joshua Hirsch also claims that the second generation experiences the parents´ trauma as an image that hurts from the inside (cf. Hirsch 2004, p. 161).

Rememory illustrates the possibility of a return of the traumatic past. Rememory and postmemory are clearly opposed to each other (cf. Hirsch 2012., p. 83). The challenge is to find a way to identify and participate by projection and allow the transmission of traumatic experiences to that extent that it does not lead to a rememory or self-wounding (cf. ibid. p. 86).

The language of the family is the language of the body, in which nightmares, sighs, illnesses, the shedding of tears and acute aches makes room (cf. Hoffman

2004, pp. 9-10). The family zone allows a transmission of trauma that blocks mere diagnostic concepts as, for instance, in therapeutic treatment. Hoffman regards her received knowledge as something completely different than professional knowledge of a psychiatrist. She is a close witness to her ancestors´ past, to their bodily symptoms, the sadness and mourning (cf. ibid., pp. 56-57). She took their suffering in and participated in it and had therefore the feeling of being able to lessen their pain and share it with them (cf. ibid., p. 58).

Children are affected by the parents´ experiences in an invisible and immediate way, in which the mental states are unintentionally and unconsciously communicated from one mind to another. Hoffman refers to this as "the transmission of trauma" or "the transmission of traumatic memory" (cf. ibid., p. 60). The second generation trauma is a vicarious trauma suffered by children of trauma victims who are known as the second generation (cf. Hirsch 2004, p. 142).

## 4.2   The Postgeneration

In 1969 the New Yorker psychoanalyst Judith Kestenberg first began examining the way the Holocaust affected survivors´ children in the aftermath. She interviewed other psychologists and found out that surprisingly little was known about the effects on children concerning their parents´ past (cf. Epstein 1987, p. 201). Psychologists did not consider the second generation, which came to therapeutic sessions looking for help, to be a phenomenon on a collective level at first. They rather treated individual cases disregarding the Shoah (cf. ibid., p. 188), until they began dealing with it more and more later on until the topic reached several academic occupational groups and Kestenberg´s assumption that the children are affected enormously by their parents´ traumatic past was acknowledged (cf. ibid., pp. 202-203).

Today, the second generation, to which communicated and received information of the past is passed on, portrays a defined community that holds meetings and conferences worldwide and which contributes to a growing field of personal as well as theoretical writing (cf. Hoffman 2004, p. xii). It is a complicated concept defined by its influential knowledge that follows from the Shoah and the Second World War. The aftereffects stick to the children of survivors many decades after the trauma (cf. ibid., pp. 25-26).

Not every member of the postgeneration has to deal with the exact same consequences of the Holocaust. Their behavior and their interest concerning the Shoah and the past differ extremely. It is important to stress that not all characteristics of possible second generation behavior can be discussed here. However, the most common features of survivors´ children and their parental upbringing will be pointed out.

The question Marianne Hirsch poses is the following: how are survivors´ children incorporated in the aftermath of traumatic events they did not witness or experience (cf. Hirsch 2012, p. 2). She argues that all of the children of survivors have certain characteristics and symptoms in common. Hirsch and Hoffman speak of a postgeneration that is constructed by the qualities that all these children share (cf. ibid., p. 4). The descendants that are directly affected by a collective trauma like the Holocaust adopt an unknown past, which can neither be known nor understood. They inherit the horrific certainty that their parents were not to meant to survive (cf. ibid., p. 34). The children share a common confusion and responsibility and are shaped by a wish to repair their parents´ past knowing that their own existence may be a compensation for the parents´ unbelievable loss (cf. ibid., p. 34).

The knowledge of a lost home, safety, a familiar environment and family members is transmitted from the first to the second generation (cf. ibid.). The transfer of such information does not take the shape of a chronological narrative, but may occur as a sudden bursting into tears, as fragmented phrases concerning the subject of the war or as mere silences. Some parents prefer to keep more silent than others. Hoffman recalls her father taking up repeated litanies, which were never further elaborated or talked about. Objects of the house had been eliminated and the past cut off (cf. Hoffman 2004, pp. 10-13). However broken, the parents´ utterances still had an impact on her. As a child she considered those simple, disconnected comments to be half real and half fairy tales, which established a norm for good and evil behavior and a standard of how the world works and looks like. Only later as an adult did she unlearn to see the Holocaust as a fundament of how the world ruled via film and literature (cf. ibid., pp. 13-15). Until then, trivial situations and behavior was generally seen by children in the context of the "norm" of the Holocaust (cf. Epstein 1987, p. 9) .

There are further analogies between Hoffman and other second generation members. The ancestors´ and parents´ suffering is in most households equated with the good and hence their pain felt during and after the Holocaust deeply respected. The pain felt by the children resonates in their bodies almost as if they had lived through the same experiences. Loyalty and hate are transmitted and deeply internalized as well. Hate towards the Germans and the perpetrators and loyalty towards parents or other victims is internalized in the minds (cf. Hoffman 2004, pp. 13-15). Even as an adult Hoffman had prejudices towards Germany and refused to visit the country due to an early imperative to hate the enemy (cf. ibid., p. 110). Some of the children fantasize about killing the persecutors of their families or Hitler himself (cf. Epstein 1987, pp. 172-173).

As the writer Helen Epstein points out, many members of the second generation consider very carefully who is trustworthy and who is not when meeting new people. The skepticism inherited from their parents is continuously acted out by the children (cf. ibid., p. 20). The space of the family is valued more than any other space regarding for instance friends or colleagues. The parents of one of Epstein´s interviewees recollects his parents´ attitude towards his friends. The parents considered them not to be as trustworthy as their son. The parents were tricked themselves by their friends during the time of their persecution and they transmitted their attitude towards their old friends to their son´s present friends (cf. ibid., p. 169). The first generation generally distrusts especially gentiles and expects their children to behave in the same manner. Children who have a tendency to rebel against their parents might insist on having a relationship or being friends with the people their parents do not approve of (cf. ibid., p. 194).

The children who grew up in survivor families had only their own perceptions and no intellectual access to political, social or historical knowledge yet. The children were closer to the families´ stories than anything else. They had to work out a meaning of the stories they were given (cf. ibid., p. 16). Reflection and historical contexts were granted later. Until then, unprocessed, unspoken and invisible psychics constituted their only world (cf. Hoffman 2004, p. 77).

The second generation grew up with the effects as they were lived in the parents´ minds.

While depicting her own childhood after the emigration of her family to New York, Epstein remembers her parents´ diverse behavior in everyday life, when she was still a child. Her mother kept her feelings and emotions hidden at almost all times while her father, who had outbursts of fury, showed his fierceness and bad temper regularly. Although there were no details revealed, the way her father ate, his teeth as well as his deformed nails portrayed what he must have experienced (cf. Epstein 1987, pp. 56-58).

Emotions as despair and fear were transmitted and not necessarily the truest representation of people or places (cf. Hoffman 2004, pp. 33-34). A certain wish to take the burden of pain, repair the losses and rescuing the parents, involving the dead relatives, accompanied the children throughout their lives. The parents frequently hoped for this rescue. They kept their hopes up, even unconsciously, that their children could save them (cf. ibid., pp. 63-64). Sometimes, the urge felt by the second generations to protect the parents was so strong that the relation switched and the children behaved as if they were the parents, not the children (cf. Epstein 1987, pp. 34-35).

Although the parents seemed strong, they were extremely fragile in reality (cf. ibid., p. 38). In everyday life they spoke stagnantly, especially in the language of a foreign country, unable to find the right words. Epstein, an American author of Czech descent and a member of the postgeneration, recalls her parents´ helplessness regarding the English language, which constituted a foreign language and an additional burden (cf. ibid., p. 154).

Although survivor children want to empathize with their parents, the first generation often keeps silent refusing to mention any details about the past. By doing so, they hope in turn to protect their children and to spare them the awful truth about the past (cf. ibid., p. 166).

Some parents reinvented themselves by having children and proving their immortality by doing so. Epstein emphasizes the parents´ habit to name their children after family members who died during the Holocaust (cf. ibid., p. 22), just as it was the case with her own name (cf. ibid., p. 52). The children often felt the duty to live not only their own life, but also the life of the late family member. In the most extreme cases, they lead the life this person would have lived if he were still alive (cf. ibid., p. 204). Kestenberg calls this a "simultaneous double existence" and emphasizes the expectation of living a life in the present as well as the past (cf. Kestenberg: *A Metapsychological Assessment Based on Analysis of a Survivor´s Child*. In: *Generations of the Holocaust*. 1982, pp. 140-141). The task of fulfilling the destiny of a lost family member involves a destroyed autonomy for the second generation since it is impossible to live two lives at the same time. The dead person, especially concerning a lost child, became therefore a hated sibling by the children born after the war (cf. Bergmann: *Thoughts on Superego Pathology of Survivors and Their Children*. In: *Generations of the Holocaust*. 1982, p. 269).

Some of the children share the same sufferings while others are less concerned with their parents´ past. When it comes to bodily and somatic symptoms, some members of the second generation are affected by eczemas or rashes signifying unconscious anxiety, which is not experienced, but inherited (cf. Hoffman 2004, pp. 65-66). Diseases as, for instance, anorexia, obsessions and various phobias may emerge due to the wish to cure the parents (cf. Kestenberg: *Survivor Parents and Their Children.* In: *Generations of the Holocaust.* 1982, pp. 100-101). The need for that is internalized to the extreme extent that bodily symptoms may appear.

Although the existence of emotions is not negated, physical pain or material objects are better adopted and comprehended by the parents than feelings, since it is difficult for many to express love with emotions and show affection directly. The children regarded their parents rather as being nervous and overwhelmed than calm and affectionate (cf. Klein-Parker: *Dominant Attitudes of Adult Children of Holocaust Survivors toward Their Parents.* In: *Human Adaptation to Extreme Stress. From the Holocaust to Vietnam.* 1988, pp. 203-206).

Parents who survived such horrific circumstances as concentration camps or persecution are constantly concerned with the issue of health. In Epstein´s composition of interviews with children of survivors, many second generation members reported that their parents thought about the children´s health and security permanently. These were their primary concerns (cf. Epstein 1987, p. 34). Additionally, the parents wanted their children to stay home most of the time in order to protect them from the environment at all times (cf. ibid., p. 167). Any separation from a family member, even if it merely concerned a child moving out from home and moving to another city for college, means a major loss for the parents. It reminds them of the loss of their loved ones and they fear they could never see them again (cf. ibid., p. 181).

Another feature some of the first generation members share is the inability to withstand their children arguing either with their siblings or with other people. These quarrels are triggered by an ignorance of how to get rid of internal emotions the children felt due to familial circumstances, as Epstein clearly remembers doing herself. The moment she felt emotions raging, she vented her anger since she did not know how to deal with those pent-up feelings and did not speak about them either (cf. ibid., p. 156).

Other parents, in contrast, picked up the topic of their suffering during the Holocaust whenever arguing with their children and emphasized their victimhood. They moved away from the actual topic of their argument and underlined how much they had to suffer stating that the cause for this suffering were the children. At times, parents blackmailed their children emotionally causing remorse and leaving them incapacitated this way (cf. ibid., pp. 286-287).

Many children do not feel sympathy for their parents exclusively, but partly also disdain and anger. They feel a burden on their shoulders imposed by the first generation. The parents expect their children to be happy and healthy all the time since they had the opportunity to grow up in times without persecution, so that the children felt they had to live their lives with an enormous burden of un-realizable expectations. They considered their happiness to be a compensation for the harm and pain of their parents. Simultaneously, the children felt they needed to suffer as their ancestors did in order to be worthy and considered as "good", because sufferers were seen as good people in the eyes of the children (cf. ibid., p. 39). Anger surfaced also in another context. Especially the younger generation always wants their parents to be strong and hence feels scorn and contempt for them when they differ from other parents considerably and are weak instead (cf. ibid., p. 68). The factor of emigration also played a crucial role for some. Many victims emigrated, especially from Eastern and Central Europe, and experienced an uprooting and another form of loss regarding their familiar environment and homes. Some did not want to stay in the places where geno-cide, personal drama and the death of families took place. Others emigrated due to hostile attitudes of local groups of people and anti-Semitism. The major part of survivors approved of new opportunities and new environments free of horri-ble associations (cf. Hoffman 2004, pp. 78-79). Emigration depicts a huge up-heaval for all people since it implies losses as friends, familiar landscapes, prop-erties and the ability to speak and understand a certain language. Due to the lack of language abilities, the isolation of a person in a new country may increase. Immigrants may not find empathy or understanding in a new country and feel inconvenient as well as fear regarding new people and new circumstances (cf. ibid., pp. 80-81). Survivors may undergo a retraumatization in these moments, especially because of the inability of other countries and cultures to be open-minded for such horrible topics like that of the Holocaust (cf. ibid. p. 85). Chil-dren from survivor families felt different than children from families without any survivor family members. Since children assimilated quicker than their par-ents and did not grow up in the same countries, cultures and circumstances as their parents, they rejected their parents´ thinking and habits to a great extent. They had difficulties understanding their parents because of their displacement from the origin country. Not only is there a temporal gap regarding the two gen-erations, but also a geographical void, which emphasizes the existence of two different worlds and different norms which are constantly counteracting. The second generation often acted as mediators between their parents and the new environment, because they had insight in and access to both worlds (cf. ibid., pp. 85-90).

The second generation often feels the need to journey back to the origin country, the place where the horror occurred and where the ancestors came from in order to be able to move on with their own lives (cf. Hirsch 2004, p. 160). Often, the parents condemned this wish believing the whole family should neither look back nor get themselves into trouble by visiting a country where once they encountered so much danger (cf. Hoffman 2004, p. 206). Exploring the countries of the parents nevertheless helps the children getting in touch with their own past and helps diminishing the gap in time as well as distance (cf. ibid., p. 220).

The second generation internalized a certain numbness and rigor, which they act out in their daily lives. The urge to evolve emotions and to dissolve the numbness is an enormous wish felt by the postgeneration at all times (cf. Epstein 1987, pp. 235-236). The children feel the need to find answers to the questions about an inherited past that they are obsessed about and owned by, but do not understand since it was never talked about (cf. ibid., p. 325).

The postgeneration depicts a group of people that did not experience life threatening situations as concentration camps or genocide. They frequently feel excluded from a world they will never know and feel a gap caused by the Shoah (cf. Fine: *The Absent Memory: The Act of Writing in Post-Holocaust French Literature*. In: *Writing and the Holocaust*. 1988, p. 41). To some extent they envy their ancestors, because they did not undergo these kinds of events where they would face the final question of existence and manage to survive an event this horrific and enormous. Contrary to the first generation, the children feel as if they have not accomplished as much as their parents. They see their lives as less worthy and less significant. The problems they come across seem to matter less or even not at all compared to the problems the parents went through. The children´s problems were seen as banal and life experiences could never be equated to those of the first generation (cf. Hoffman 2004, pp. 68-69). The parents themselves dismissed their children´s problems indicating their insignificance or minor importance. The outstanding wish for a comparable achievement as the parents´ survival determined the children´s lives (cf. Epstein 1987, pp. 155-156). At times, the postgeneration either fantasized about their own survival or created real situations in which they had to prove to themselves and to others that they would be able to survive as well (cf. ibid., p 214).

The grown-up members of the second generation see their parents at times coping better with their traumatic past than the children themselves. They seem to be less depressed or afraid. Therefore, some of the parents wonder at their children's poor state of mind, especially if they kept silent about their past in order to protect their children and not pass their sadness and depression on to them. The sympathies between parents and children however often increase and the incomprehension diminishes once the children grow up (cf. Hoffman 2004, pp. 182-183).The relationship changes along with the growing age of the children and often the shame felt at the beginning shifts to admiration and pride concerning the parents´ abilities and strength for survival (cf. Klein-Parker: *Dominant Attitudes of Adult Children of Holocaust Survivors toward Their Parents*. In: *Human Adaptation to Extreme Stress. From the Holocaust to Vietnam*. 1988, pp. 214-215).

The second generation has to face constant claims and imperatives while growing up. Their needs are weighed down by the parents´ needs continuously. Due to an enormous need for presence and attachment by the first generation, the children take care of their parents wishing for own autonomy at the same time. They wage a war within themselves between self-sacrifice and self-interest (cf. Hoffman 2004, pp. 96-97).

Klein-Parker´s research, a study done by another second generation member, deals also with the impact of the parents´ trauma on their children due to personal fate and her own relationship to their parents. She interviewed several members of the postgeneration and discovered the dominant and opinionated attitude of the parents. Most of the children communicated a superficial relationship, in which the parents constantly gave advise trying to guide their lives. The second generation tried to evolve an interest for the topics the parents liked discussing and realized their parents´ limited openness and tolerance towards many concerns (cf. Klein-Parker: *Dominant Attitudes of Adult Children of Holocaust Sur-*

*vivors toward Their Parents*. In: Wilson/Harel/Kahana: *Human Adaptation to Extreme Stress. From the Holocaust to Vietnam.*1988, pp. 193-199). Their controlling behavior and intrusive voice lingering in the children´s minds hindered them from creating an own identity (cf. ibid., pp. 208-209).

The fight with the haunting of shadows instead of fixed experienced realities, which according to Hoffman is a much more difficult task (cf. Hoffman 2004, p. 66), could be stopped as soon as the members of the second generation find a way to free themselves of the invisible past. They have to decide on a life without those phantoms and confront themselves with an uncanny or yet unknown past in an imaginative manner. This includes going through imaginative scenarios, through imaginative images of lost objects or persons so that they acknowledge the realities of their legacy as realities (cf. ibid., pp. 73-74).

Hoffman proposes an unfreezing of internalized images and stories the children of survivors carry with them. She herself internalized the image of an attic her parents hid in during the war, which powerfully occupies her internal imagery of the past. Regardless of the fact that the attic in her mind may not correspond to the real attic that existed, it still captures her mind. These once received images are difficult to correct once they are integrated (cf. ibid., pp. 193-194), but they should be weakened so that the knowledge about the past is not reduced to transferred knowledge only. She approves of an enlarging of knowledge involving own perspectives (cf. ibid., pp. 197-198).

The second generation experiences proximity to the consequences of traumatic suffering. Hoffman suggests a separation from the feelings that accompanied the transmission of trauma as for instance rage, loss or gratitude, so that the past can be separated from the present and mourning can be put to an end (cf. ibid., pp. 278-279).

Although the question of a God who would let the Holocaust to happen is always present (cf. Epstein 1987, p. 26), the second generation does not necessarily feel the aftereffects of the Holocaust on a religious level. They are proud of the Jewish people´s survival and the consequences of the Shoah determine an identity construction rather than a religious bonding. They feel they belong to a certain group of people (cf. ibid., p. 116). As Joshua Hirsch indicates, second generation memory of past traumatic events "[...] actually organizes major aspects of one´s identity" (Hirsch 2004, p. 150). Just as has been pointed out earlier, not all of the parents or children share the same emotions or behave in the same way. This also concerns the aspect of religion. Some of them turned away completely from Judaism, some turned to it (cf. Epstein 1987, p. 117). Epstein recounts that she herself was not religious as a child, because she did not believe in a God that could allow such a disaster. She went to school on Sundays in order to learn about Jewish history, religion and language, but did not want to do that voluntarily. In order to protect her mother from disappointments, she continued her Jewish education. Together with other members of the second generation (cf. ibid., p. 123), Epstein did not reveal her true thoughts about her unwillingness to go to this school to protect the first generation (cf. ibid., pp. 142-143). Many of the children only identified with Judaism in the context of the Holocaust. The traditions or rituals concerning religion were not practiced regularly (cf. ibid., p. 180).

The aftereffects of the Holocaust and the indirect received knowledge still haunts the postgeneration. It has an impact on their psyches, although they did not experience it themselves. Nevertheless, it does determine the lives of the children disregarding the different countries and cultures they now live in (cf. Hoffman 2004, pp. 27-28).

Although not experienced, the Holocaust and their parents´ trauma effects the children´s lives, so that conversations about WW2 and Jewish persecution by the Nazis are never impartial or without bias (cf. ibid., p. 101). The second generation is left with the difficult task to comprehend their parents´ past without debasement or idealization (cf. Kestenberg, Judith S./Kesternerg, Milton: *The Background of the Study*. In: *Generations of the Holocaust*. 1982, p. 61). The survivor´s guilt that was transmitted from parent to child (cf. Bergmann, Maria V.: Thoughts on Superego Pathology of Survivors and Their Children. In: *Generations of the Holocaust*. 1982, p. 305), needs to be abandoned. The children need to break free from it in order to create a new life of their own that is separate from their parents´ lives and embrace personal freedom (cf. ibid., pp. 308-309).

Since the second generation grew up in different countries all around the world, they have had difficulties establishing a community in which they could act together as a political body. The internal emotions of confusion and a search for identity is shared by most children (cf. Hoffman 2004, pp. 245-246). As adults, the second generation expresses the need for a belonging to a group with the same experiences. Hoffman considers the second generation to be "[…] a community based not so much on geography or circumstance as on sets of meanings, symbols, and even literary fictions that it has in common and that enables its members to recognize and converse with each other with a sense of mutual belonging" (ibid., p. 28). In the next chapter, the literal work produced by the postgeneration and the way the children deal with the topic of the Holocaust and their parents past will be examined in detail.

## 4.3   Second Generation Art

Since the preoccupation with the Holocaust is still increasing, the Shoah has captured public consciousness and as a historical event acts as a cultural phenomenon (cf. ibid., pp. 156-157). The second generation feels the need, probably neither more nor less than the first generation, to put the past behind, which can be achieved via shared mourning and commemoration. This remembering of the past allows an alleviation of pain on a collective as well as individual level.

According to Hoffman, fictional as well as reflective literature helps contemplating on the topic of the Holocaust (cf. ibid., pp. 161-162).

Second generation artists have been producing movies, novels and literature (cf. ibid., p. 3). The literal work, which includes fiction, art and memoirs aims at representing a closeness to the pain and depression of victims of extreme and historical trauma (cf. ibid., p. 34). Survivor testimonies, poems, diaries or oral reports mirror the extremity and the conditions existent during the Holocaust (cf. ibid., p. 163).

Sharing narratives of or about victims implies breaking a silence the survivor might have wanted to maintain. Authors of postmemorial works find themselves in, as Hirsch states, a "paradoxical space", in which they express what the traumatized person may not have wanted to share (cf. Hirsch 2012, p. 90). Hoffman argues that the literal second generation now reckons not only with the Holocaust, but also with the relationship to their ancestors who survived the trauma. There is on the one hand this horrific past that now becomes a memory and which needs to be analyzed, interpreted and comprehended. On the other hand there are also emotions towards the parents that re-emerge as well as the thought of autonomy, repressed feelings and phobias that still haunt the children (Hoffman 2004, p. 181). With the help of literature, the second generation is able to preserve the past, which they feel they have an obligation to do. Writing and articulating the own experience extends psychotherapy in many cases. Memoirs and art created by survivors are written from memory while postmemorial art talks about this memory. What is emphasized in these works by children are challenges and uncertainties of proper recall. They look for personal history and engage themselves in discovering family secrets, creating stories out of broken phrases and establishing own identities (cf. ibid., pp. 187-188). Klein-Parker refers to this as "self-therapy" meaning second generation members writing poetry, prose and other literature pieces in order to deal and understand the aftereffects of the Shoah (cf. Klein-Parker: *Dominant Attitudes of Adult Children of Holocaust Survivors toward Their Parents*. In: *Human Adaptation to Extreme Stress. From the Holocaust to Vietnam.* 1988, p. 211).

Second generation art or, as Zeitlin argues, "vicarious witnessing", whether in the form of memoirs, diaries or chronicles, is composed of a zone of traumatized memory (cf. Zeitlin 1998, p. 6). The one writing about the past without participating in it becomes an active presence, who reenacts the past and pursues: "[…] an obsessive quest to assume the burden of memory, of rememoration, by means of which one might become a witness oneself" (ibid.). The memory is approximated to the extent that the postgeneration feels as if it witnessed the event itself.

In order to put the past behind, it needs to be commemorated. What is being remembered of the past depends on the literature that portrays this past. The produced literature gives shape to the past events that took place and shows people what is to be remembered. Literature, which is an available medium in culture, forms the way we perceive and commemorate the past. James Edward Young assumes that due to this fact the literal as well as the historical truth cannot be separated completely. According to Young, the literal descriptive and the factual historical interpretation flow together (cf. Young 1992, pp. 13-14). People rely on mediating texts for historical knowledge, but these texts should not be the only source for historical investigations. Young claims: "[…] die Signifikanz und die Bedeutung, welche die Texte den Ereignissen geben, spiegeln oft nur wieder, wie diese Ereignisse damals von den Opfern begriffen wurden" (ibid., p. 16). The historical truth and the form in which it is communicated are connected and the events should be recognized within the form of their representation (cf. ibid., pp. 19-20).

Literature about the Holocaust involves constructions of a reality which is not able to portray the world realistically. Constructions of this kind do not mimic the world. What is constructed are versions of reality. Although authors of Holocaust literature are expected to be realistic in their works, this aim cannot be achieved. Literature has an interpretive character and does not perform any direct reproduction of reality (cf. ibid., pp. 36-38). Rothe also argues that any kind of literal representation offers a communicated, limited, and interpreted reflection and mere idea of reality (cf. Rothe 2011, p. 85).

Second generation art, as for instance diaries and memoirs, reveals that somebody witnessed certain events, that he passes his knowledge to other people and that, ultimately, he finds meaning in the transmission of his knowledge. These literature pieces include testimony on these several levels (cf. Young 1992, p. 39-40). What should be valued is the importance of the combination of testimony and interpretation and not the insistence of factuality in literal testimonies (cf. ibid., pp. 43-44).

In memoirs, writers wish to mediate a powerful past with the main goal to implement the remembered emotions and feelings. The manner in which the author remembers those, is very crucial. Memoir writers are involved with very personal as well as sociopolitical aspects in their works (cf. Kaplan 2005, p. 43).

Memoirs, in which the author wants to testify, represent a form of literature which creates authenticity as part of invention (cf. Young 1992, pp. 46-47). The writer presents his version of reality post factum knowing the results of an event he witnessed. Past experiences are seen not in the moment of their happening, but after their occurrence. The author foregrounds certain details of the experience and by doing so, he arranges the events in a certain way marking a significance which was not present at the time of its happening (cf. ibid., pp. 57-59). A retrospective interpretation of events takes place. The memoir demonstrates the act of writing itself and not particularly historical accuracy (cf. ibid., pp. 68-69). It intertwines authentic declarations with less authentic ones concentrating on the authority of the teller (cf. ibid. pp. 90-105).

This group of Holocaust literature that includes autobiographies and memoirs calls for historical veracity by distinguishing itself from mere historical writings and demanding the reader´s belief in the verisimilitude it presents at the same time (cf. Lang 2000, pp. 20-21).

Claiming that voices of witnesses should not be disregarded, James Edward Young proposes the term "received memory", with the help of which he emphasizes that history is always received is a certain way. Listeners and readers are affected by survivor stories or historical recordings and their effectiveness is ascribed to their statements about the past. The effectiveness and the mere telling of the past can therefore be both restored to the historical record, since nobody, not even historians, can cut themselves off from being effected while writing down history. The second generation´s perception of the past therefore shapes the past also (cf. Young 1997, pp. 42-43). According to Young, nobody can separate himself from his own point of view, time or context when writing about the Shoah (cf. ibid., p. 33). The memory of the survivor should not be considered less worthy since the mixing and the exchange of historical accuracy and the victim´s memory create meaning in the understanding of the past (cf. ibid., pp. 37-38). The unreliability that goes hand in hand with survivor stories is still a part of history. When knowledge is passed on from generation to generation, not only memory is transferred but also inaudible pauses or personal points of engagement that constitute the journey to the past. Received history marks real as well as imaginative involvement (cf. ibid., pp. 40-42). It describes what happened and how events are remembered (cf. Young 1998, p. 697).

The passing down of memory becomes problematic since there are certain gaps and absences involved, which becomes visible in literature (cf. Elmwood 2004, p. 692). The literal second generation is confronted with the task of imagining an event they have not experienced, which they have to reconstitute and assimilate into their writing. Fine refers to it as bringing a story into being out of history (cf. Fine: *The Absent Memory: The Act of Writing in Post-Holocaust French Literature*. In: *Writing and the Holocaust*. 1988, p. 41). Literature allows a distance from trauma, which would otherwise be out of reach. In spite of the guilt of not having been involved in the traumatic event, the second generation needs to fill the blank spaces with their imaginative creation. They have to find their own words in order to describe a past they have no access to. The "absent memory", meaning a memory the postgeneration cannot know, but must not forget (cf. ibid., p. 56), is portrayed in the writings by gaps of memory that cannot be filled (cf. ibid., pp. 42-44). If the writer speaks on behalf of the dead, he takes the burden of guilt for making up memories that are not his own, but by openly revealing the guilt connected to the act of writing, he integrates the blank voids into his text (cf. ibid., pp. 55-56). By filling the gaps or leaving them blank if it is wished so by the author, he articulates a story for himself and is able to put the past behind.

In the next chapter, we will look at the protagonist in Art Spiegelman´s *The Complete Maus* and the way he is affected by the familial transmission of trauma. The manner in which he deals with postmemory as well as his behavior as a postgeneration member will be examined.

# 5. Postmemory in Art Spiegelman´s *The Complete Maus*

## 5.1 Possession by History and Antagonistic Behavior

Art Spiegelman´s *The Complete Maus* portrays the challenges and issues of those born after the trauma of the Shoah (cf. Banner 2000, p. 4) and involves the strong desire to gain information about the past they did not experience. The consciousness that the memory of this past is actually located in the present is emphasized in Spiegelman´s black and white graphic narrative (cf. Hirsch 2012, p. 40).

The interactions between father and son, the first and the second generation, demonstrate familial postmemory and depict the way the father´s memory becomes the son´s postmemory (cf. ibid., p. 41). The work´s focus lies on Art´s struggle to comprehend the continuous effects of Vladek´s past (cf. Elmwood 2004, p. 717).

In spite of Art´s wish to get to know the past he did not experience himself, the conversations between Vladek and Art are not always successful and the interaction often uncooperative (cf. Elmwood 2004, p. 691). Spiegelman himself states that his parents never spoke about their past in any coherent or understandable way (cf. Spiegelman 2011, p. 12).

At the beginning of the comic, in the prologue, the reader is confronted with a scene taken from Art´s childhood. Art is playing with his friends in New York in 1958. They are roller-slating when suddenly Art´s skate comes loose and he falls. His friends run away and Art, in his frustration, turns to his father (cf. Spiegelman 2003, p. 5). Vladek asks why Art is crying and his son tells him what happened. Vladek stops his occupation and tells him: "FRIENDS? YOUR FRIENDS?...IF YOU LOCK THEM TOGETHER IN A ROOM WITH NO FOOD FOR A WEEK...THEN YOU COULD SEE WHAT IT IS, FRIENDS!..." (ibid., p. 6). Vladek does not show any empathy or affection for his son undermining his problem and sadness at the same time. Not only does he communicate his negative attitude towards his friends in general, he also does it via a broken utterance, which Art cannot understand. The broken fragments are used without a context and especially for a child these utterances are not comprehensible since they lack any explanation. Art does not see the whole context of Vladek´s experiences yet and does not understand why he would think so. Only later Art and reader get to know Vladek´s bad experience with supposedly good friends who were in fact only concerned with themselves (cf. ibid., p. 216). Here, the message lacks any context and does not form a coherent story. Art´s problem is considered to be less significant compared to Vladek´s experiences with his friends during the Holocaust.

As an adult, Art is eager to learn more about the Holocaust and convinces his father to tell him about his past. He starts by asking Vladek to reveal stories about Anja: "I WANT TO HEAR IT. START WITH MOM…TELL ME HOW YOU MET" (ibid., p. 14). Art is interested in his own origin, in the people that made him and the moment his closest family came to be (cf. Young 1998, p. 679). Vladek is sitting on an exercycle and while pedaling he starts his story with another former girlfriend of his and ignores Art´s request. Art however insists again and reminds Vladek of Anja. Vladek, with squinted eyes and anger, refuses it persisting on wanting to tell it his way (cf. Spiegelman 2003, p. 16). Visually, this lack of reciprocal working together is portrayed as well. Art is situated in the upper half and second panel on the page while Vladek is located in the middle of it. They do talk to each other, but they do not face each other on the same level.

When, according to Spiegelman, Vladek first starts pedaling: "[…] into the past […]" (Spiegelman 2011, p. 209), his image is displayed over several panels, which altogether form one big picture. In the middle of the page the reader finds Art situated between the father´s arms. Right above Art´s head one recognizes

Vladek´s tattooed number he got in Auschwitz (cf. Spiegelman 2003, p. 14). Art is embedded within the upper part of Vladek´s body and the exercycle. This image indicates the capture in which Art finds himself. He is enclosed in his father´s telling of the past as well as the instrument that metaphorically takes him there. The fact that the tattooed number is located right above Art´s head marks the immediacy Art feels regarding Auschwitz and the Holocaust.

Art does not seem interested in other stories Vladek wants to share. When the father is telling his son about an eye operation he had, Art does not really listen and shows his indifference: "UH-HUH- YOU TOLD ME ABOUT THAT" (ibid., p. 42).

Art is overwhelmed with Vladek´s story and occupied by his narration. The depiction of Vladek sitting on his exercycle takes up almost the entire page. Art, in contrast, is very small and almost hidden (cf. ibid., p. 14). Vladek´s personality and his narration of the traumatic past he experienced visually take the most space. Throughout the whole graphic narrative Vladek is portrayed more often and takes up most of the room. Although at first Art calls his father´s memories "material" and merely concentrates on the writing of his book, his interest for the topic of the Holocaust increases more and more (cf. Banner 2000, pp. 141-142). Later on, as he gets deeper and deeper into his father´s narrative, he is anxious to listen about the war and sits in front of his father like a little child (cf. Spiegelman 2003, p. 47). In the following panels, Vladek takes up more and more space while Art makes room for his father, physically as well as metaphorically for his narrative. His mind is occupied with the past more and more.

During another visit, Art and Vladek take a walk and go to the bank together. Art picks up the topic of their last meeting and asks his father to continue his narration. Vladek narrates about the time in 1943 and the village in Sosnowiec. The street in Poland Vladek is referring to is depicted at the bottom of the page (cf. ibid., p. 107). Art and Vladek are placed within this panel, but are portrayed without borders. It looks as if they were walking on the street Vladek is talking about. This depiction illustrates the investment Art takes. He participates in the telling about the past and inscribes himself into Vladek´s story. Due to the lack of the borders the distinction between the past and the present is clear. It is evident that Art did not witness this situation himself. There is rupture when it comes to Art´s knowledge about what has occurred back then. He is not able to know every detail, face, conversation or place. Nevertheless, the continuity, passed on from father to son, and the ongoing aftereffects of the past become visible.

During his narration Vladek emphasizes the importance of religion several times. He claims that during the war he prayed every day and practiced his Jewish belief (cf. ibid., p. 56). Although Art does not know much about Judaism and is not very religious (cf. ibid., p. 59), he is nevertheless also depicted with a mouse mask. Just as Vladek and all the Jews in the graphic narrative, Art claims his Jewish identity and wears a mouse mask all the time. Since second generation members often do not lead religious lives, they identify with their Jewish ancestors especially when it comes to an identity formation. Art chooses to identify with his father and his ancestors and actively puts on a mouse mask in order to express this identification. Berlatsky argues that humans actively choose their identities. The use of the animal masks demonstrates this act (cf. Berlatsky 2003, p. 133). Later on in the comic narrative, Art is wearing a mouse mask the way that the reader sees his human face behind it (cf. Spiegelman 2003, p. 201). This sequence underlines the choice that Art has when it comes to the identification with Judaism. He does not relate to Art´s religious belief, but chooses to identify with the traumatic past of his ancestors. Also Art´s wife Francoise chooses to be represented as a mouse and wishes to take part in the exercise of a collective memory that forms Jewish identity (cf. Mulman: *A Tale of Two Mice: Graphic Representations of the Jew in Holocaust Narrative*. In: *The Jewish Graphic Novel. Critical Approaches*. 2008 p. 90). They are part of a collectivity which establishes its group consciousness on the fundaments of the traumatic experience of the Holocaust.

At times, Vladek´s younger version and Art resemble very much, which makes Art´s identification with his father even more visible (cf. Spiegelman 2003, p. 14).

Identification with the parents or ancestors may be so intense that the child´s autonomy and own life story risks to be displaced. Especially in survivor families the affective force felt by the children may overwhelm their own lives and over-identification may lead to a replacement of their own lives by their parents´ lives.

Art is strongly affected by his parents´ past. He feels depressed after hearing Vladek´s whole life story (cf. ibid., p. 201) and is possessed by the history he did not witness. He admits to his wife Francoise that he had had nightmares as a child about S.S. men coming into his class room pulling all the Jewish children away (cf. ibid., p. 176). He would fantasize Zyklon B coming out of the shower instead of water and he feels envy, because his parents both lived through the Holocaust and Auschwitz. He himself did not experience anything so horrific that would be just as awful. He wishes he had been there to witness the horror himself, which is a typical feature of survivor children who are deeply affected by postmemory. Art feels guilty that he had a better and easier life than the rest of his family. Even his late brother, whom he never met, witnessed the traumatic event. Art feels guilty that he is the only one from his family who had a pleasant life and feels left out (cf. ibid.). The dead brother Richieu is like a ghost-brother to Art, whom he envies the love and affection of his parents he had never experienced himself. Art´s mother and father had a photo of Richieu, whom Art regarded as an ideal kid for having had the same experiences his parents had. Since they did not have a photo of Art, he started to feel anger and hate for Richieu, who became a hated sibling and a constant rival. For Art, Richieu´s photo is a statement of reproach and he feels as if he could never be as ideal as Richieu (cf. ibid., p. 175). In fact, the dead perfect brother is a negation of Art, a rival whom he cannot compete with. Richieu will always be aligned with their parents due to the same experience while Art is not able to fill Richieu´s shoes, which he somehow feels he should do (cf. Elmwood 2004, p. 704). Even the fact that Vladek confuses Art with Richieu and calls him by this name on his death-bed foregrounds Richieu´s everlasting presence. This again proves the internalized thinking of how suffering can be characterized as a feature of good people whereas the lack of it as a characteristic of the bad. Art feels bad for not having suffered at all.

After the mother´s suicide, Art depicts his feelings in the comic strip "Prisoner on the Hell Planet" in which he also underlines Vladek´s reaction to the incident. In spite of the guilt and sadness Art feels, he is the one that has to comfort Vladek and be there for him. Art is expected to calm him although he himself is overwhelmed by his emotions (cf. ibid., p. 103). The parental obligation seems to have switched here. Vladek behaves as he was the child revealing his despera-tion openly while Art controls his sadness and is there for his father: "**I** WAS EXPECTED TO COMFORT **HIM**!" (ibid.). The switched roles of the parent and the child, which often occurs in survivor families and which children fre-quently report, is emphasized in Art´s short comic strip. In one of the panels the reader sees Vladek hiding behind Art´s shoulder and clinging to them (cf. ibid.). The demand to save and protect the parent is clearly visible. What needs to be kept in mind is that the depiction of this scene mirrors Art´s way of seeing his father. He feels the pressure laid in his shoulders by Vladek, who longs for sup-port and encouragement. Art puts his arms protectively around Vladek as if he was his child and not the other way around.

Art desperately pressures Vladek to find Anja´s notebooks that talk about her life and past. Although Vladek first mentions their existence, he ignores Art´s wish and changes the subject by distracting Art again and again. Whenever Art mentions the diaries to his father, Vladek does not respond to this until much later. He does not admit that he destroyed them. He merely states that those diaries do not exist, but he does not mention the reason for that (cf. ibid., p. 86). After Art´s statement that he desperately needs them for the book he wants to write, Vladek immediately changes the subject: "COFF! **PLEASE**, ARTIE, STOP WITH THE SMOKING. IT MAKES ME SHORT WITH BREATH" (ibid.). Vladek´s eye positioning in this panel tells the reader that he does not want to deal with the subject of Anja´s notebooks. He wants to get away from it and pushes it away, just as his hands suggest. Not only does Vladek not want to deal with it himself, but he also wants Art to be distracted from Anja´s leftovers. He works against him and blocks Art´s wish to get in touch with her story as well. He flees from his own past and by destroying the journals he takes the possibility from Art to deal with his mother.

Vladek ignores Art´s asking for Anja´s diaries on purpose, which Young calls a "prescient delaying tactic" (cf. Young 1998, p. 686). In his desperation, Art burned Anja´s notebooks and by gaining time and not admitting to this action, Vladek omits dealing with Art´s reaction to it. He ignores Art´s asking several times throughout the graphic narrative and distracts his son by talking about other issues (cf. Spiegelman 2003, p. 107). Vladek is traumatized to the extent that he does not want to accept any other stories and realities than his own.

Due to the lack of these notebooks, Art has no access to Anja´s story (cf. Zeitlin 1998, p. 11). Her identity cannot be recaptured and Art´s relationship to her cannot be retrieved anymore (cf. Berlatsky 2003, p. 106). When Vladek eventually tells Art of the journals´ destruction, Art gets furious and calls Vladek a murderer (cf. Spiegelman 2003, p. 161).

He murdered Art´s wish to build a relation to his mother´s past, which he inevitably strongly desires. His relation to his mother and her past cannot be formed anymore.

According to Spiegelman, the most crucial moment of the graphic narrative is the sequence, when Art is sitting at his desk with dead corpses lying at his feet. He feels guilty because of the success his work brought him and he feels that he somehow profited from genocide (cf. Spiegelman 2011, pp. 145-146). Not only is Art´s possession by history apparent due to the dead bodies and the tower reminiscent of Auschwitz that is visible through the window, but also the comparison between Art´s and Vladek´s lives is portrayed (cf. Spiegelman 2003, p. 201). He alternatively reports the reader about Vladek and his own life stating a clear difference especially focusing on the work each of the men was occupied with: "Vladek started working as a tinman in Auschwitz in the spring of 1944…I started working on this page at the very end of February 1987" (ibid.). The juxtaposition of both lives shows Art´s need for comparison. Additionally, this comparison shows the consequence of Vladek´s trauma. If Vladek had not experienced Auschwitz in 1944, Art would not have written his work many years later.

Art is affected by the chaos of emotions and the imagery that was passed on him. He thinks in the norm of the Holocaust. After his father´s death Art feels depressed and is overwhelmed with his feelings. Banner emphasizes the aspect of Art´s ongoing, inherited and vicarious trauma in the moment he sitting at the desk surrounded by dead corpses (cf. Banner 2000, p. 163) and spots the link between father and son. We see Art thinking about the offers he received to turn his book into a movie and then a voice, which could be assigned to a television employee, informs Art that they are ready to start the project. We read: "Alright Mr. Spiegelman..We´re ready to shoot!..." (ibid.). Spiegelman did not use a neutral verb, but it sounds as if someone said it to Spiegelman Senior, who found himself various times in dangerous situations where one would want to shoot him (cf. ibid., p. 163). The verb has completely different meanings since it can be found in different contexts here. On the one hand, the shooting concerns Art´s possible television project, on the other hand it is referring to Vladek´s past. This link underlines the impact Vladek´s past has on Art.

Not only does Vladek work against Art, but the son also thwarts his father´s behavior. Although Vladek does not want Art to include the stories about Lucia in his book, a girl he was seeing back then, Art does it anyway (cf. ibid., p. 25). His father does not want such private things to be revealed and Art promises to not write about that. As can be seen in the graphic narrative, he breaks that promise. Art speaks in Art´s name, reserves his right to talk about someone else´s issues. Much later, Art feels guilty of speaking about other people´s lives and the horrible events they experienced, which he did not. He claims: "IT´S SO **PRE-SUMPTUOUS** OF ME" (ibid., p. 174) and feels inadequate to write a book in which he tries to make sense out of Auschwitz. Not only is he concerned with trying to find meaning in the relationship with Vladek, but also with the unknown past, which is what all survivor children try to accomplish.

He also states that there is so much in the past he cannot begin to imagine (cf. ibid., p. 206). This statement emphasizes the rupture that Art has to experience, since he not able to know everything that happened in the past. There are always gaps and holes that will accompany him due to the lack of knowledge about an internalized past that he did not witness himself. Since survivor children need to find a way how to claim the past and traumatic event for themselves (cf. Elmwood 2004, p. 718), Art needs to claim Vladek´s past and turn it into his own story. In the next chapter, the way Art manages to accomplish this will be examined.

## 5.2 Forming a Version of the Past

Art is deeply affected by postmemory and is emotionally involved in his father´s telling of the traumatic past. The connection to it is made by imaginative investment, projection as well as creation. As Art points out earlier, he is not able to start imagining what happened back then and how difficult and stressful it must have been to live through such horrific situations like being in Auschwitz (cf. Spiegelman 2003, p. 206). Several pages later Vladek tells Art that although both do not know Anja´s experiences for sure, Art can however: "[…] IMAGINE WHAT SHE WENT THROUGH (ibid., p. 226). This utterance works like an encouragement for Art to envision the past and create a version of it. In this sense, Vladek helps Art to create a story of his own that is necessary for his own identity formation. Although Vladek is the one that destroyed Anja´s journals, he nevertheless tells Art pieces of her story and delivers partly what Art needs. The holes and gaps that come with the lack of these notebooks are filled through imagination and creation. The same process takes places when it comes to all the other gaps that Art needs to fill. Art himself admits that there is: "[…] SO MUCH I´LL NEVER BE ABLE TO UNDERSTAND OR VISUALIZE. [:::] SO MUCH HAS TO BE LEFT OUT […]" (ibid., p. 176).

Life without phantoms is made possible by imagining the unknown past and by searching for dialogues and conversations. With the help of his father, Art invents the dialogues his father had with the people in the past and imagines the places he used to be. The reader cannot be sure if Vladek reports all the dialogues and delivers all the information that is incorporated into the graphic narrative. One might assume that there are certain details Art constructs in order to create a whole image of the past for himself. The reader is confronted with situations as, for instance, a short interaction between Vladek´s father and Richieu, in which the grandfather gives a cookie to his grandson that his daughter baked (cf. ibid., p. 91). This detail is not told by Vladek above the panel. This interaction may as well be invented so that Art can imagine what could have happened during this meeting.

Art also invents Vladek´s thoughts when they are sitting in the car after picking up the hitch-hiker. He imagines what Vladek is thinking in Polish at this point, which additionally emphasizes Art´s high degree of imaginative investment in the comic (cf. ibid., p. 259).

The son is creating a whole story with invented dialogues in order to make a story for himself. He creates facial expressions, imagines how places could have looked like and due to the limited and incomplete knowledge of the past fills the gaps in his father´s memories. He produces events and situations he is not able to know.

In search for autonomy and an own identity, Art creates a version of the past for himself. The process of writing is crucial and makes this identity formation possible. Although Vladek´s story takes up most of the space and he seems to be in the focus, the work deals mostly with Art´s need for a story and the filling of gaps in order to achieve that. Art insists on a coherent and chronological story and asks Vladek to deliver that (cf. ibid., p. 228).

Eventually, Art creates and imagines the past to the great extent that implies the invention of the father figure himself. The way he portrays Vladek is not necessarily the real Vladek that existed. Vladek´s depiction in the graphic narrative derives from Art´s imagination. The conversations, places, the wardrobe, gestures and mimic of people are all the outcome of Art´s imagination. These aspects, especially the depicted people and most importantly Vladek, are portrayed the way the author specifically intended.

With the help of Vladek´s descriptions and narrative, Art forms a version of the past. The father contributes to this formulation by showing Art photos and snapshots of the past (cf. ibid., p. 273) and by drawing a sketch of a bunker he hid in (cf. ibid., p. 112). Partly, he helps Art to comprehend the past.

Additionally to his father´s reports, Art is also open for other sources and un-freezes internalized images by incorporating external information that is not coming merely from Vladek. The author includes charts that show objects and their value for exchanges in Auschwitz (cf. ibid., p. 224). This also shows Art´s investigation of the past and shows how important it is for Art to understand the past circumstances in the concentration camp. He includes a map of Auschwitz (cf. ibid., p. 166), of Poland back at that time (cf. ibid., p. 62), includes a instruc-tion of how to fix shoes the way Vladek used to do it in Auschwitz (cf. ibid., p. 220) and makes a time table for himself to understand the succession of events that Vladek reports (cf. ibid., p. 228).

Art constructs his identity with the help of Vladek´s memories (cf. Berlatsky 2003, p. 120). Spiegelman uses his father´s memory, but simultaneously blurs binaries and engages himself in a postmodern aesthetic by discussing the logical value of memory, history and identity (cf. ibid., pp. 125-126). Spiegelman in-terweaves oral survivor testimony, biography, autobiography, since Art repre-sents Spiegelman´s in an autobiographical sense (cf. ibid., p. 104), and graphic narrative (cf. ibid., p. 126). It is a difficult task to assign *The Complete Maus* to one single genre (cf. Banner 2000, p. 5), but since art and history are mixed and oral testimony as well as creation and projection used, an intersection of both areas takes place (cf. Zeitlin 1998, p. 6). Spiegelman requested a re-consideration when his work faced a classification problem and moved from fic-tion to non-fiction Best Seller Lists back and forth. Finally, it moved to the non-fiction area. Spiegelman´s work involves a scholarly as well as aesthetic way to investigate the past (cf. Doherty 1996, pp. 69-70), but due to an accurate inves-tigation of documents, places and events, Spiegelman himself considers his work of art to be non-fiction (cf. Spiegelman 2001, p. 46). He visited Auschwitz and examined all the information he needed carefully (cf. ibid., p. 57). History, meaning the reconstruction of people, events as well as places, is factual and mixed here with identity and memory (cf. Berlatsky 2003, pp. 126-127). Since memory expands the consequences of historical events, history and memory exist reciprocally (cf. Elmwood 2004, p. 717).

The reality fiction dichotomy in *The Complete Maus* implies a meta-fictional self-reflexiveness, in which the literary making of it is emphasized (cf. Berlastky 2003, p. 130). There is no universal truth, but Vladek´s narrative as text works a truth. According to Berlatsky, these metafictional and postmodern methods characterize Spiegelman´s work as postmodernist fiction (cf. ibid., pp. 136-140).

History and memory co-exist and Young considers *The Complete Maus* to be a model for received history, in which the traumatic event of the Shoah and the transmission of it are depicted (cf. Young 1998, p. 669). The father´s narrative and Art´s reception of it are portrayed at the same time (cf. ibid., p. 676).

In the prologue the reader finds the date of Art´s first memory right at the beginning. The abbreviated term "circa" underlines the imprecise and unfixed feature of memory (cf. Spiegelman 2003, p. 5). The exact dates are not relevant in this testimony. What matters is the meaning of this memory, as Banner points out (cf. Banner 2000, p. 135).

Spiegelman supports the co-existence of memory and history, which work alternately and yet simultaneously and portrays this in his graphic narrative. Although the existence of an orchestra in Auschwitz has been documented, Vladek does not remember it. Spiegelman allows the possibility of two versions by placing a panel with the depiction of the orchestra and one without it (cf. Spiegelman 2003, p. 214). The testimony of an eye-witness, even if it lacks factual accuracy, equals historical documentation (cf. Elmwood 2004, pp. 698-699). Another sequence depicts the possibility of a man being Jewish or German. There are two panels that respectively show him with a mouse and a cat mask (cf. Spiegelman 2003, p. 210).

Vladek himself emphasizes that his memory may be inaccurate and that he may not remember or know what happened completely: "I DONT **KNOW** IF THIS IS HOW IT WAS WITH MANDELBAUM [...]" (ibid., p. 195).

Not the reproduction of an accurate reality is Spiegelman´s goal, but the act of writing that allows Art to create a version of reality, which forms his identity. The post-factum identity he achieves is possible via the process of writing, in which Art finds meaning.

At the end of the graphic narrative the reader sees Vladek´s and Anja´s tombstone with their dates of birth and death on it. We also see Spiegelman´s signature and the period of time he was occupied with the writing of the narrative (cf. ibid., p. 296). Spiegelman uses this depiction as a reminder that this book is made by a person that remembers the past with the help of this narrative (cf. Spiegelman 2011, p. 234). Young argues that this signature and the years signify that Spiegelman completed the process of writing and his creative act came to an end (cf. Young 1998, p. 682). Not only is Art´s need for a version of the past and his identity formation completed, but this sequence also shows how Art is literally engraved by his parents´ past" (cf. Mandaville 2009, p. 243). As soon as the tape recorder stops, Vladek´s story also comes to an end (cf. Banner 2000, p. 170). Vladek tells Art to stop the recorder since he is tired from talking and thinks that: "[...] IT´S ENOUGH STORIES FOR NOW..." (Spiegelman 2003, p. 296). Art found the answers to his questions, knows that he belongs to the Jewish community that remembers the Holocaust and he feels as one of them. The description and story about memory as an active act of writing formulates identity. There is nothing more Art needs to know or hear.

## 6. Trauma and Postmemory in Helen Fremont´s *After Long Silence*

### 6.1 The Permanent Silence of the First Generation

Helen Fremont´s memoir *After Long Silence* portrays a couple of Holocaust survivors and their two daughters as well as the way the events of World War II
and the parents´ experiences affect the lives of both generations.

After having been raised as a Roman Catholic, Helen and her sister Lara discover their parents´ Jewish identity. Both her mother and her father decide to keep
their past a secret and never speak a word about it. Helen, driven by the need to
learn about a past she did not experience, uncovers traumatic events her parents
went through during Russian as well German occupations in Poland. She learns
about her mother´s and aunt´s survival and escape to Italy and her father´s flight
from a labor camp in Siberia. Helen discovers the truth about her roots step by
step and encounters her mother´s emotional instability, her father´s determination, her aunt´s decisiveness and her own need for an identity and belonging.

Helen´s family goes through horrific situations during the war and experiences
continuous traumatic events together as well as separately. Resident in Lvov,
which included one third Jews, one third Poles and one third Ukrainians in prewar Poland (cf. Fremont 1999, p. 163), the family experiences Russian occupation in 1941 before the arrival of the Germans. Kovik, considered dangerous for
the Soviets due to his negative opinion about the Soviet ideal, is at first imprisoned for some time before being sent off to Gulag, a Soviet labor camp, where
he spends six years far away from family and home (cf. ibid., p. 130). During his
incarcerations undertaken by the Soviets he does not have contact with his family, does not receive any letters and does not know if they are still alive or not
(cf. ibid., p. 221). Additionally to his disconnection from the world, he goes
through mental and physical abuse. He loses weight, sleeps in a crouched and
uncomfortable position and is constantly involved in fights (cf. ibid., p. 150). He

gets beaten and loses his teeth (cf. ibid., p. 155). Some fellow inmates break his arm, which bents a weird angle whenever he moves it (cf. ibid., p. 225).

Kovik, a self-employed family doctor (cf. ibid., p. 7) of iron will and strong character, suffers from PTSD after his prolonged and chronic abuse. It affects him at a later date, when his daughters Helen and Lara are already grown up. He is repeatedly captured by a traumatic memory which forces him to relive the trauma he experienced. Helen herself sees that her father has probably never gotten out of the Gulag, because it possesses him continuously and appears suddenly and unexpected. A prolonged trauma like Kovik´s imprisonment stays with the victim for the rest of his life (cf. ibid., p. 223). Helen recalls the moments in which the past resurfaces again clearly. On Christmas, Kovik opens a gift from a patient of his and finds two stitched belts. He falls into a deep silence and with an absent mind declares that these belts would have been the most wonderful gifts in the camps since people had the opportunity to hang themselves and end their misery with the help of these items (cf. ibid.). Kovik acts out his trauma and relives the situations back then. The belts remind him of his trauma and take him back to his past experience, which he utters in a fragmented manner. Kovik repeatedly falls into a silence, in which he finds no words for his trauma, but fragmentarily delivers pieces about the Gulag. One day, Helen brings her roommate over to her parents´ home for barbecue. While preparing the food, Kovik falls into one of his silences and starts telling Helen´s friend about the Gulag and how he and the other prisoners were starving. They found a rotten tomato and when a fellow inmate tried to eat it, a guard shot him in the head. Kovik had to step over him and pretend that nothing happened (cf. ibid., p. 224). The tomato on the grill, reminiscent of the rotten tomato back then, portrays the intrusion Kovik suffers from. He relives the traumatic situation once again and does not have the distance to it yet that would allow an incorporation of his trauma into his life. Although he never talks about it (cf. ibid., p. 225), the left arm that was broken by the prisoners, is also a reminder of the Gulag at all times. Whenever Kovik looks at that arm, his memories about the past might be re-awaken.

Helen finds an article in which her father tells the newspaper about the issue with his broken arm (cf. ibid., p. 226). He reveals the whole story to strangers, but does not talk to his daughter about it. Victims often have less difficulties sharing their story with people they do not know than with their families since they do not know how their reaction is going to be. Afraid of an uncomprehending and condemning attitude, Kovik disapproves of telling his daughter about his painful and degrading experience.

When his arm first gets broken and the possibility of an incorrect healing is immensely high, Kovik asks during his incarceration five strong men to pull his broken arm and set it right. He orders them to do it several times until he is content with the results (cf. ibid., p. 229). His strong will and determination continue on until the present day. His strong willpower, which the Gulag seems to have taught him, proceed until many years after his escape from the camp. Helen remembers his father´s will to clear the snow on Christmas from their drive way, which turned out to be a difficult task with the constantly falling snow. Kovik, driven by his determined decision to complete this task, falls down several times and breaks his ribs. He does not stop until it is done (cf. ibid. p. 231). Kovik still lives by the norms of his past captivity. His determined will to survive still controls his behavior and only by completing the task and reaching the goal he establishes for himself is he able to survive. After an arm operation after the war, Kovik exercises his arm with determination to be able to play the violin as he used to do it before (cf. ibid., p. 226). The Gulag taught him to fight for his survival and by working hard Kovik not only survives the traumatic experience, but he survives every day in the present.

Kovik suffers also from hyperarousal, which is characterized by the anticipation of danger as well as the survivor´s aggressive behavior. He has outbursts of fury and exclaims utterances in such a manner that the daughters get scared and suppose their father must have seen something disturbing as the rolling of tanks on the street (cf. ibid., p. 123). Kovik´s way of acting out is manifold. He does it by raising his voice with an alarm tone in it or by getting extremely nervous in front of a policeman years after the war, as Helen recalls. She remembers his father´s sweat breaking out and his inability of normal breathing in front of the officer (cf. ibid., p. 194-195). This policeman reminds Kovik of the past and of the perpetrators that kept him imprisoned. He cannot distinguish between the present and the past and gets tensed and nervous due to a possible repetition of the dangerous and traumatic situation of the past. He might be afraid of another physical or mental abuse.

Helen´s mother, a slender and supple woman, likes rearranging nature in her garden for hours. She cleans the house and takes care of the family (cf. ibid., pp. 9-10). Having experienced traumatic events of World War II, an incarceration in a camp (cf. ibid., p. 7), the loss of her parents and the disappearance of her fiancé, she is also in pain due to her past and suffers from PTSD.

Helen talks about her childhood memories and recollects her mother´s behavior and delayed response to trauma many decades after the war. Helen, brought up as Roman Catholic, used to practice the Lord´s Prayer in six different languages due to her mother´s major language abilities. Helen used to pick out a specific language and she and her mother said the prayer together. Helen used to enjoy this habit of theirs since she got to spend some time with her other alone (cf. ibid., pp.11-12). What Helen considered to be a simple ritual, turns out to be the mother´s way of preparing the daughter for possible dangerous situations. Having lived through Russian and German occupations, in which language skills could save lives, the mother wants to give her daughter the ability to save herself just in case. Helen herself underlines her mother´s belief in the possibility of hiding their Jewish identity with the help of other languages: "What I didn´t understand was that my mother was equipping me with the means of survival: proof of my Catholicism to anyone in a dozen countries" (ibid.). The mother, having been a translator during occupation and being offered several jobs, was able to save herself and her family and earn some money (cf. ibid., p. 178). Helen´s mother confuses the past with the present and, as a form of acting out, prepares her daughter for a possible return of danger. She still thinks in the norms of the past, in which it was dangerous to reveal one´s own identity. Many years later, Helen´s mother is scared to tell anyone that she and her family is Jewish and works on the image of a typical happy family for cover (cf. ibid., p. 14), afraid to be noticeable to neighbors, friends or even family who sometimes could not be trusted. Helen´s father himself claims years after the war in 1993: "´You´re safer *not* trusting your friends´" (ibid., p. 342). The changes of being betrayed and deported were high back then and this attitude and thinking still lingers in the mother´s mind when she prepares Helen for unsafe situations like these.

Helen´s mother survives World War II by using a false name, false documents and adopting the identity of a Catholic girl named Maria. She escapes from the Nazis, dressed as a soldier from Italy (cf. ibid., p.18). The fact that she still covers her true identity brings out the mother´s high degree of traumatization. She does not even admit to her real name she had before the war. The trust in a safe environment is gone and she is disconnected from herself, her true identity, as well as society, which she not does open up to. She stubbornly sticks to her thinking and Helen herself realizes that: "To this day I don´t even know what my mother´s real name is" (ibid.). The mother´s traumatization goes to such lengths that she does not reveal her real name to her closest family members decades after the traumatic experiences.

The unspeakability and the lack of language that captures Helen´s mother possesses her at a later date and is repeatedly released through her wound. Her daughters confront her again and again with the truth once they find out about their Jewish descent, but the mother does not respond to it at first. She shrugs her shoulders and her eyes squeeze. She dismisses it quickly: "'I doubt it [...] But I don't know" (ibid., p. 23). Later on, she behaves and replies in a more aggressive manner: "'What difference does it make whether you're Jewish or Catholic or Protestant or Buddhist?!'" (ibid., p. 26). After having been confronted multiple times, she throws up her hands, reminiscent of the way one would defend himself from an unpleasant topic, and raises her voice claiming: "'I told you, I don't want to talk about it! [...] It's too painful for me! I cannot do it!'" (ibid., p. 41). Helen's mother, whom the implied author refers to as Batya in the memoir, but whose real name is actually still unknown, wants to eliminate her traumatic knowledge from her consciousness. There is no description of the past, but a complete denial. She is constantly irritated and she turns from anger to bewilderment every once in a while. After finding out what happened to the grandparents and how they died, Lara and Helen feel the need to share this information with Batya. She herself does not know what happened to them and demands this information from her daughters (cf. ibid., p. 42). There is a sudden change in behavior and her anger turns to bewilderment. Helen reveals the grandparents' destiny, but her mother does not seem to listen. She only repeats that she wants to know what happened, but actually does not let this information sink in (cf. ibid., p. 43). She is ready to hear about her parents' death in the concentration camp in Belzec, but immediately refuses to hear about the death of her other relatives (cf. ibid., pp. 204-205). She shields herself from it and does not want to hear more than she can take. This behavior is typical of trauma victims who want to know about the past and be ignorant at the same time. Helen's mother might be too afraid to get exposed to the truth directly and protects herself from knowing too much. The mother's emotional and contradictory behavior depicts the impact that the traumatic loss of her parents had on her.

The daughters share a common wish to discover the truth about their family. Their mother reacts with a deep anger to this need, which she is not able to modulate. The girls try to make the mother understand their reason for investigating. She does not see the true reason behind their actions, but a constant danger. She suffers from repeated flashbacks and nightmares and past memories haunt her, so that even her childhood and the poor circumstances of her family re-emerge (cf. ibid., p. 47). She is plagued by the same dream over and over again, in which the police come and take her house away (cf. ibid., p. 194). She relives the event and suffers from intrusion. Instead of a cautious approach, Helen´s and Lara´s mother is thrown into the past she so badly tries to escape from. She resists any form of possible closure claiming: "'I have no number. I wasn´t in the camps. I was never in Auschwitz'" (ibid., p. 58). She clings to this statement emphasizing that she cannot be a survivor due to this fact (cf. ibid., p. 58). The mother´s goal is to prove her detachment from the Holocaust, but her statement is actually true. She, de facto, did not survive it, but remains a prisoner for the rest of her life. She did make it through the horror physically, but she did not mentally, because she is still reliving it in the present.

At a certain point, Batya decides to give in and tells her daughters about her past. Fifty years after the war (cf. ibid., p. 198), the mother reacts to her experiences with a belayed response. The battle between remembering and forgetting still rules Batya´s mind (cf. ibid.). The will to deny the event and to proclaim it can be clearly seen in her behavior.

Although she partly begins to articulate a story for herself, she still does not admit to ever having been involved much in religion. She claims her family was not very religious back then, which Helen does not believe (cf. ibid., pp. 50-51). Batya is not able to fully let go of her denial.

The tension and danger that Batya was exposed to ranges from the beginning of the war in 1939 until the end of it. The prolonged state of fear and dread make the victim go into a constant state of alert after the event. Batya used to be tough and strong with a determined will to survive (cf. ibid., p. 125). Her trauma most likely changed her personality forever. She is fragile and gets easily disturbed. Helen asks herself if her mother changed after her experiences (cf. ibid.). The stories Batya tells her daughters about herself describe a young woman that Helen does not seem to recognize. The prolonged trauma of the war experiences changed her personality. She used to daydream joyfully, but after the war she becomes a sharp and silent person (cf. ibid., p. 297). The mother, being a wily character, used to keep herself together, but as soon as this form of defense is not of use anymore, PTSD sets in and changes Batya into a fragile image of a woman.

She is impatient and gets annoyed when someone interrupts her story about the past (cf. ibid., p, 136). Her lips quiver and she is crying whenever thinking or talking about her late family members (cf. ibid., p. 2). There is no distance from the past at all, but she is constantly acting out her unuttered trauma. The reader learns that Batya suffers from night fears and a repetition compulsion, in which she flicks the light on and off several times, checks under the bed to see that nobody is there, peeks behind the curtains, under the desk before returning to the lights again. This night routine, which according to Helen takes a lot of time (cf. ibid., p. 158), portrays Batya´s struggle to find meaning and order in her life. She does this routine because she wants to make sure that she is safe and because she fears that somebody is going to get her. Additionally, she creates a zone of security in the bedroom she does the routine in, so that she practically feels safe there when she does not in the world outside.

During the war, Batya allows her parents to leave and stay with her aunt Checha Godja in another town. Batya´s mother insists that they go without her. After their departure, Batya has difficulties sleeping and eating (cf. ibid., p. 212). She blames herself for letting her parents go alone, especially because she knew she would never see them again (cf. ibid., pp. 215-216). She feels more and more depressed. Her guilt only increases within the years after she learns that this was the last time she saw her parents alive. The survivor guilt and the feeling of shame still haunt her. The moment she learns that her parents do not respond to her letters she writes from Rome after she escaped from Poland is the moment when the silence begins (cf. ibid., p. 254) and Batya´s depression starts. This silence continues on to the present day.

When Helen´s and Lara´s parents emigrate to America in 1959, the separation that Batya and her sister Zosia go through, gives both sisters a hard time. They thought: "[…] they would never see each other again; separation meant extermination in their experience […]" (ibid., p. 297). The emigration that is about to take place is reminiscent for both sisters with the separation of their family members who died during the war. Afraid to lose each other forever, they confuse the past with the present and dread a return of the same scenario.

Batya is completely captured by the silence she and Kovik as well as her sister Zosia stick to. Helen assumes that her parents dwell on it for their own as well as their children´s sake. They want to protect Helen and Lara from the truth (cf. ibid., p. 31) and also protect themselves from knowing too much. Another confrontation with the horrific and traumatizing past they went through is to be omitted. The zone of unspeakability and the black hole, in which there are no words for describing the past and the victims just simply fall into, protect them from another encounter with trauma, but make a working through impossible at the same time. As a friend of Helen´s parents points out: "'They have had very hard lives. We have all suffered a great deal […] We have lost everyone, everything, and the same is true with your parents'" (ibid., p. 37). The trauma that was given birth to by loss, death and danger is too overwhelming for the parents and a confrontation with the truth and their Jewish identity extremely painful.

Batya´s sister Zosia is presented as a very strong, independent fast-moving character, who as a young girl knows how to present herself in public in contrast to her sister Batya, who likes to sleep late, read books and is more of a passive character (cf. ibid., p. 67). During the war, Zosia takes care of the whole family. Once, she dresses up and goes out with a Soviet soldier so that her father does not get arrested for hiding state property after the Russian occupation in 1939. She saves him from deportation (cf. ibid., pp. 115-116). When her parents are unemployed, Zosia is the one that brings home food and makes deals with merchants (cf. ibid., p. 118).

Between Russian and German occupations, there were no laws present. Lootings took place as well as rape all around the place (cf. ibid., p. 146). In the middle of this scenario, Zosia manages to get her sister out of this massacre claiming that she herself is Aryan and an Italian citizen due to her marriage with an Italian attorney (cf. ibid., p. 77). She insists that her sister Batya is therefore also an Aryan and saves her (cf. ibid., p. 164). This event is extremely traumatic to both sisters, but they react differently to it years after that. While Batya remembers this situation clearly, Zosia does not remember anything (cf. ibid., p. 147). She suffers from total amnesia. She does not remember her sister´s real name either (cf. ibid., p. 324). According to Danieli, victims at times forget their lives before a traumatic event and protect themselves from it by doing so. Zosia eliminates the traumatic circumstances from her consciousness as well. Zosia keeps silent about her past just like Batya and Kovik. She does not say anything to her son Renzo about her Jewish identity, but keeps it a secret from him and invents another false story about her family and the death of Renzo´s grandparents (cf. ibid., p. 317).

Zosia gets furious when she is told that Kovik is willing to reveal the truth to his daughters on their 18th birthday. She vetoes it and negates his decision completely (cf. ibid., p. 279). Just like Batya, Zosia does not want to expose her nieces to danger, but wants to protect them. She does not want anybody to know the secret of their Jewish descent in order to not be exposed to possible racism and anti-Semitism.

Zosia, being fanatic about Judaism and pro-Israel (cf. ibid., p. 308), is passionate about the topic of the Holocaust and has always read much about it (cf. ibid., p. 314). However, the formulation of the traumatic event does not take place. Helen tells Zosia that she and Lara know about their Jewish identity. Zosia does not react aggressively and is not as upset as Batya when she was confronted with it (cf. ibid., p. 321).

Still, Zosia does not go into detail about the past. A few days after the confrontation in Rome in Zosia´s apartment, she yells at Helen and accuses her of having been spying on her (cf. ibid., p. 332). She does not understand Helen´s wish to belong to the Jewish community, but confuses the past with the present. She is very sensitive about Helen´s intrusion into her past. She shouts at her stating: "'You´re worse than Hitler! […] you´re doing it for no other reason than sheer cruelty!'" (ibid., p. 333). Zosia´s feeling of security is demolished, she does not trust anyone and is disconnected from society. She categorizes Helen as an enemy, who interferes into her personal life. A retraumatization occurs, in which she falls back into a deep depression (cf. ibid., p. 339). She fills her life with bridge games and social activities in her free time (cf. ibid., p. 325) and is occupied with her daily tasks, but withdraws from close relationships like the one with her niece Helen and refuses to let the traumatic past back into her mind.

Helen hears the stories about World War II and feels its impact on her own life. By listening to their stories Helen discovers that she is vicariously traumatized by her parents´ past: "[…] for some reason the story about my father in Siberia was weighing on me " (ibid., p. 16). When she talks about this at a young age with a friend of hers, she starts fighting back tears, but feels an unexplainable wish to talk about it with another person (cf. ibid.). Listeners of traumatic stories may feel confusion and bewilderment and Helen also feels the emotional burden when she thinks about her parents´ suffering or her father being weak with his broken arm in the Gulag when she normally considers him to be strong and powerful (cf. ibid., p. 226).

The parents decide to keep their true identity hidden from their children and the rest of the world (cf. ibid., p. 8). The issue of the war and their experiences remain silent. Their loss of family members, their property, their homes and a feeling of security and safety contribute to the severe condition of PTSD. After emigrating to the United States, which forms an additional upheaval for the first generation and includes additional loss of a familiar environment and language abilities, the parents change their last name to "Bocard", a name that does not sound Jewish at all (cf. ibid., p. 300). The past gets erased and together with the memory of it, their past identities also get deleted. Although Kovik sticks by his wife´s promise to not talk about the past, he is ready to reveal more than her. He talks to Helen in an excited whisper about his experience with the Catholic Church as a boy and his blessings from it when he was sick. He makes sure that Helen´s mother does not hear him (cf. ibid., p. 83), and shows his willingness to talk to the world about this partly. In 1987 he writes a memoir of six hundred pages about his experiences in the Gulag, which Helen´s mother refuses to read (cf. ibid., p. 278). Kovik wants his daughters to read it, which emphasizes his wish to proclaim the past and his need for an audience. The fact that he talks to a newspaper about it also underlines his urge to find a listener or an audience. He looks for opportunities to have conversations about it, but waits for Batya to leave before he says something about their Jewish identity (cf. ibid., p. 279). He is the one who wants to tell his daughters the truth when they turn 18, but eventually he promises his wife to not say anything (cf. ibid.). Kovik desires a formulation of his experiences and creation of the story, which would lead to a reconstruction of his trauma story. The formulation would give him a meaning and the required distance he needs for a successful healing, possible to some extent after complex trauma. His wife, demanding complete silence from her husband, keeps him from performing this act and from recovery. The truth is not acknowledged, but eliminated from consciousness.

In 1965 Kovik registers his wife and daughters in family therapy, but nobody really talks about the past there (cf. ibid., pp. 157-159). The family insists on keeping the silence. The family's refusal to talk avoids rebuilding safety, reconstruction of trauma story or reconnection to the outside world, in which one finds toleration, empowerment and trust.

The first generation, including Kovik, Batya and Zosia, refuse to attend a family reunion (cf. ibid., p. 348) and withdraw from relationships, especially those that would connect them to their Jewish past. They are unwilling to accept their loss, but block the future and stick to their disconnection from themselves and society. Since they are forced by Helen and Lara to reveal their past, they are not in control of the process of healing. Although there is a willing listener to their stories that the daughters constitute, the second generation does not accept their silences (cf. ibid., p. 41). They push the first generation and force them to narrate their past and a retraumatization takes place. What is needed instead are repeated encounters with the past, in which the first generation controls the pace of the narration while feeling safe and protected. Only then, working through would be possible.

## 6.2 A Hindered Quest for an Unknown Past

Helen Fremonts's *After Long Silence* presents a powerful work that deals with "[…] the quest for a hidden past or the reckoning with the scars and wounds left in the wake of the Holocaust […]" (Hoffman 2004, p. 188). The aftereffects of World War II are visible in the behavior of the first as well as of the second generation. The transmission of trauma and its impact on Helen 's and Lara's lives become apparent in their quest for a personal history.

Parental transmission of trauma takes place within a familiar space, in which the language of the body works significantly. Additionally, fragmented answers are given without any coherence. When Helen asks Batya about her own mother during the war, she glances away and replies: "'Oh, she died'" (Fremont 1999, p. 1). She does not go into detail about the past and does not deliver any context, in which Helen could understand her statement. Helen knows something bad must have happened to her family and her ancestors, but she does comprehend the whole story. Her mother´s lips quiver and she starts crying when she talks about the bomb that took her family´s lives away with a shaky voice (cf. ibid., p. 2). She tells her daughter a story that is made up and totally false, but the emotions Batya feels concerning her parents and the past are still true.

Batya´s body language is full of tightness. Her wrists hold tightly to the table edge and she takes the position that would remind one of a fighter in a boxing ring. Her jaw gets clenched and her mouth compressed (cf. ibid., p. 40). Helen gets fragmented information lacking chronology from her mother since she cannot ascribe the body language to a story or context. She takes these signs in and accepts them comprehending something must have happened, but does not know exactly what.

Whenever Helen asks for details, because she does not understand the circumstances, her mother dismisses her either by a sweep of her hand or by lips movements (cf. ibid., p. 258). Her mother does not reply or give the needed information, but just ignores the fact that Helen does not understand how her mother could go to the German military-supply department for food as a Jewish girl. Since Batya spoke German, nobody suspected her of anything (cf. ibid.). There are certain details and contexts Helen does not know. Although Helen desperately tries to gain more information about the past, her parents make it difficult and try to hinder her from it. Whenever Helen and Lara try to confront her mother with their Jewish descent and ask her whether it is true, Batya does not admit the truth. She becomes hostile when Helen tells her that most of her friends are Jewish and she feels she is, too (cf. ibid., p. 25). She shows the girls a postcard she wrote in 1943 to their aunt Zosia instead to prove they are Catholic and reinforce her argument that the issue with the Jewish descent is simply not true (cf. ibid., pp. 26-28). Not only does she ignore her daughter´s wish to talk about the past because of her own trauma and fear of being confronted with it again, but also because she does not want her daughters to find out the truth and accept their descent when she herself is not able to do so. She is traumatized to the extent that she does not want to accept another version of the story than the one she invented for herself.

The fragmented answers Batya gives include ruptures and gaps Helen does not know and cannot ever learn. Her mother shrugs Helen´s question off several times and Helen feels there are still pieces of her story missing (cf. ibid., p. 50).

One time, Batya tells her daughters about some leather ski boots of hers, but gives no further information about them. Helen points out how: "The past was always like this, an empty space in our lives, a gap in our conversations, into which our mother tumbled from time to time, quietly, without warning" (ibid., p. 145). The daughters know there is something dangerous about this topic, but they cannot grasp the whole picture (cf. ibid.). The mother, throwing a single image in the conversation, does not try to explain the anything further. After having been asked details about the boots, she does not answer, but acts as if she does not know what the girls are talking about. Helen and Lara know they are not meant to see the context of the whole story (cf. ibid., pp. 145-146). The pieces that are missing are meant to stay that way. The daughters are not able to understand all the details of her mother´s story and accept the incomplete narration to some extent.

The daughters both feel the continuous impact of their parents trauma. When they were children, Helen recalls how their mother would not stand when the girls were having arguments. She fell down to her knees and wished to have died together with her parents. The daughters turned to perfect children then feeling completely disarmed (cf. ibid., p. 21). Their father also made the girls feel bad about arguing claiming: "'For this I starved sic years in the Gulag?'" (ibid., p. 157). Typical of trauma victims, the parents expected the girls to be happy all the time not causing additional unneeded pain. The daughters being still children felt the expectation, stopped their argument and turned into good children not knowing why they caused their parents pain with their behavior.

With an imperative tone, the mother tells her daughter Helen what to do and how to live, which gives Helen a hard time developing her own identity. Even when Helen tells her mother that she is gay and that she has known that for a longer period of time, Batya does not seem to accept Helen´s truth, but reasons her into thinking it through (cf. ibid., p. 257). Helen herself feels that her autonomy and identity are under her mother´s custody. She subconsciously wants to please her mother not able to actually develop her own wishes and her own way of living. Due to her mother´s traumatic experiences she does not want to cause her any more harm. That is why she decides to keep her sexual orientation a secret from their parents (cf. ibid. p. 175) and actually imitates their way of thinking. She is also silent about her truth in order to protect her parents. This mirrors the way her parents kept silent about their truth not wanting their daughters to get hurt neither.

Helen is deeply affected by postmemory from the very beginning of her childhood. She has never understood the way it affected her thinking: "I had been living my life with flawed vision, stumbling in the dark, bumping into things I hadn´t realized were there" (ibid., p. 31). There were unuttered invisible threats which lacked explanation and in order to gain information and be able to understand the incomprehensible parts of the past, Helen and Lara express the wish to go to Jerusalem (cf. ibid., p. 46), the heart of the Jewish community, to explore their past. This wish is not understood by Batya and she dismisses it with disgust emphasizing how she is against their plans (cf. ibid.). As most Holocaust survivors and trauma victims, Batya regards her daughters´ wish to go to Jerusalem as an unnecessary danger. She would want Lara and Helen to keep silent about being Jewish the same way she does it and by going to Jerusalem they do not keep the silence, but explore their past. The danger of exposing their true identity that could lead to deportation back then is still lived out by Batya, who still lives by this norms and considers this trip to be a possible threat to the daughters. She is afraid of losing her children.

When a Holocaust survivor organizes a trip to Galicia for survivor families both daughters want to travel to the original country of devastation, in which their parents´ experiences took place (cf. ibid., p. 47). It takes Batya several weeks to get used to this idea and she finally understands that she cannot prevent her daughters from going. She is nevertheless afraid her daughters might encounter the same danger as she did. The first generation completely breaks off with the past by emigrating to the United States.

The equalization of past and present also involves a continuous demonstration and transmission of nervousness and fear. The parents communicate to their daughters the negative feelings they have concerning Eastern Europe and the past. They lack an understanding and calmness. These negative emotions take the risk to be adopted by the daughters. Their own lives take the risk to be replaced by the parent´s attitudes and emotions and autonomy is likely to be subdued.

Helen is named by her late paternal grandmother, whom her father admits to have hated. After her death though he decides to give his mother another chance and names his daughter after her (cf. ibid., p. 83). This is another obstacle for Helen who wants to develop an own sense of autonomy and identity. She feels she has to live the life of another person survivors and has to correct the mistakes her grandmother did. The duty Helen feels upon her shoulders to live a double life prevents her from acknowledging her own independent life.

Helen feels the shadows of her mother´s past at all times. She recognizes the parallels but also the differences between them. The special intragenerational relations between sisters is visible and emphasized so that identification takes place to a certain degree. Whenever Helen discovers a detail of the sisters´ lives in the first generation, she contrasts the lives of the second generation to it and compares both. Zosia´s and Lara´s college lives are juxtaposed and it becomes very clear how different those are (cf. ibid., pp. 68-69). Zosia went to college in the midst of danger, violence and strict quotas for Jews, which did not allow her to go to the University of Lvov (cf. ibid., p. 68). Lara, in contrast, did not have to face these circumstances, but enrolled in a college she wanted to go to and lived in a modern room. Lara had more than just one suitcase full of clothes and a jar of her mother´s jam, as Zosdia did (cf. ibid.). Lara had her properties loaded in a Chrysler that would not shut because it had so many clothes and things loaded in it (cf. ibid., p. 69). The juxtaposition of both sisters and the easier circumstances in Lara´s life become evident. Helen also mentions the similarities between Zosia and Lara and emphasizes their energy and restless character (cf. ibid., p. 106). Helen herself feels more like her mother, who requires less attention and likes to keep herself entertained (cf. ibid.). Both sisters identify with the first generation here to a certain degree. The strong bond between Zosia and Batya however is something that the second generation tries to live up to, but fails along the way. They try to copy the model of ideal sisters the first generation exemplifies, but Helen and Lara feel they are not able to accomplish it (cf. ibid., p. 106).

The comparison between generations takes place throughout the whole narrative and is still present in Helen´s and Lara´s minds. The political and historical distance between the generations becomes very visible and marks a clear difference between them. The first generation is tied together by silence and extreme war experiences, which Lara and Helen can never achieve. What the second generation sisters can achieve though relates to their need to find out about the past, as Helen herself realizes (cf. ibid., p. 161). The wish to go on a voyage of discovery and reveal the parents´ silence glues them together and the young sisters tend more and more to get away from a burden and expectation laid on by the older sisters. Helen and Lara start comprehending that the thinking of: "[…] whichever pair of sisters had the stronger bond would win" (ibid.) does not need to be pursued anymore. Helen does feel closer and closer to her sister the more the story unfolds, but not the way she is expected anymore. Helen breaks up the image of a complete identification with her mother also when she states that already at: "[…] the age of twelve, I sensed that my romantic life would be completely different from my mother´s" (ibid., p. 94). This statement forecasts Helen´s knowledge about being a lesbian, but also foregrounds the different way of living that is not comparable to her mother´s not only in a historical sense, but also in a romantic sense.

Children of survivors often feel guilty for having had an easier life than their parents. Helen also, as the last born in the family, feels the burden of guilt on her shoulders. She received from others, who sacrificed their own needs for her without expecting anything in return (cf. ibid., p. 96). The fact that she received and never had to give up anything herself makes her feel guilty. Helen admits she hates herself for having been spoiled and protected (cf. ibid., p. 202).

Due to this guilt, Helen starts imagining her parents difficult past in her Twenties in 1982 and feels the need to prove she can live through difficult situations as well. She decides to take a five-mile hike stuffed with mountaineering skis in her backpack, a sleeping bag and tent on her head (cf. ibid., pp. 128-129). She lacks sleep and food and addresses herself to the task of conquering the hike herself, which is reminiscent of the way her father would set tasks for himself for his own survival. Suddenly, she falls on an icy ledge and crashes down falling on her face into a brook. While trying to crawl out, an image of her parents´ past emerges. Not able to imagine what kind of brutal situations they must have gone through, she questions herself and her ability to survive what they survived. With a sinking sense of self-worth Helen complains: "Nothing I could ever do would be enough, I thought" (ibid., p. 129). The suffering that in Helen´s mind is categorized as good and heroic, is an act she strives for. She wants to prove to the world that she is able to do the same thing as her parents. This is the reason she completes law school, but decides not to become a lawyer, but to teach English and science in southern Africa instead. Her parents are shocked, but Helen, driven by the need to experience physical and emotional poverty again, goes abroad to a country in which political and racial circumstances give her the severity that she needs (cf. ibid., p. 293). She proves her strength for survival and, by choosing similar and difficult circumstances, tries to copy her parents´ experiences. She lives there without any access to heat, electricity or plumbing. Not until much later does she realize that she imitates her parents survival (cf. ibid., pp. 293-294). She has to learn a new language and get used to new customs just like her parents had to when they emigrated (cf. ibid., p. 294), which meant an additional emotional upheaval and loss of a familiar environment for them. Her parents, being furious at her for leaving them (cf. ibid.), associate her decision with another loss they find difficult to accept. Helen returns home after having a rupture of ligament in her knee. She has surgery back home, which resembles her father´s behavior and his experiences with his broken arm (cf. ibid., p. 294). Helen, satisfied that she proved everyone she could go through similar situations as her parents, does not give in before reaching this goal. She might have proved her will to survive, but nevertheless copies her father´s way of thinking to the very last moment. This act shows the deep aftereffects her father´s experience and talking about them has on Helen´s way of thinking and her own behavior.

Helen experiences panic attacks and takes drugs prescribed by a psychiatrist (cf. ibid., p. 201). The bodily symptoms that children of survivors suffer from often derive from their emotional instability and inability to deal with phantoms they do not understand. The accumulation of emotions and impossibility of talking about them in their families cause negative effects on their bodies. Not only is Helen affected by the past, but also her sister Lara ,who suffers from an eating disorder as a teen (cf. ibid., p. 187). Not able to deal with her emotional state, Lara keeps herself busy with her looks and figure.

From the beginning, Helen and Lara have problems understanding what happened in their parents´ lives. The transmission of trauma in the familial space is the first knowledge the girls receive about the unknown past. They knew their parents came from a foreign dangerous country, had experienced the war and also that they had been in concentration camps (cf. ibid., p. 7). The girls grew up with the story that her grandparents died because of a bomb. There were no other sources of knowledge, but the stories of the parents. Helen only knew two possibilities that could happen during war. Either one could get killed by a bomb or be imprisoned in concentration camps (cf. ibid.). The transmitted knowledge constituted the first that the daughters internalized deeply.

Seeing many tattooed numbers on wrists of other survivors, who speak with Polish or German accents, and being shown off to them (cf. ibid., p. 20) does not lead to any explanation, but further confusion in Helen´s world. Helen, presented as a proof of victory over Hitler, does not understand the way her family and she herself is implicated in this victory (cf. ibid.). However, she spends much time out of the house already as a child and pretends she has another family that does not include survivors (cf. ibid., p. 158). Like many survivor children Helen feels disdain and anger for her family, because they are different from other families she knows. She has difficulties comprehending the emotions her parents communicate. She locks herself up in her room (cf. ibid.) not being able to interpret their feelings, wishes and expectations.

Typical of trauma victims, the parents have a superficial relationship with their children. Helen remembers that her parents never asked their daughters about their personal lives. They did not mention anything about partners, children or the future (cf. ibid., p. 176). Both arre very clingy, as Helen points out. Helen however shows her desire for freedom and individuality and wishes to go out with her friends most of the time (cf. ibid., p. 177).

At the age of 8 Helen already feels the need to write her parents´ story some day (cf. ibid., p. 343). Although she does not know much about the past at this point, she already wants to piece together the story of her parents´ past which contributes also to her own. She is taken in by the things she does not understand and is pushed by the need to find out more. By exploring the story of her ancestors, Helen knows she can find her own story and get in touch with herself: "Theirs was a barely spoken narrative that led, I somehow felt, directly to my soul" (ibid., p. 344).

## 6.3. Breaking the Silence

Helen and Lara both insist on hearing the story about their parents´ past and share a common deep wish to fill unknown gaps. Finally, their mother gives in and decides to have a conversation with her daughters about the past. She delivers chunks of her story, which help Helen to see the past more clearly: "What she told us that day would eventually help me piece together the story of her life" (ibid., p. 50). The reason for searching the past and piecing together fragments of stories is the immense desire for one´s own identity. In the stories the daughters are told, they have to deal with rupture and gaps since they cannot know every detail, because they themselves did not experience these traumatic situations. Helen admits that she never knew how her father escaped from Siberia. The details of it are absent and unknown. She once received general information and knew that he escaped by jumping on a train (cf. ibid., p. 8). The way he did it and how it must have occurred turns into a story with the help of Helen´s imagination: "I pictured him dangling from his own good arm, long, tattered legs swinging an arc each time the train banked a curve" (ibid.).

Finally, the parents agree to go over maps showing prewar Poland and tell their daughters where their hometowns were so they can go and visit those places (cf. ibid., p. 51). After a long time of persuasion, the parents give in and work with their daughters. They help them find an image of the past they need for their own identity. There are a lot of details Helen does not know and the reader cannot be sure if someone told her or not. The facts Helen does not get told, she imagines. She creates dialogues, imagines places, invents behavior and looks she will never get to see. Although Helen does not know much about her maternal grandfather due to missing photos or descriptions of him (cf. ibid., p. 66), she imagines how he could have behaved and what he was like: "Moshe wandered into the kitchen, newspaper in hand, and nodded to Kovik" (ibid., p. 119). The imaginative investment and creation allow Helen to create a version of the past for herself. She admits not knowing exactly what happened, for instance at her aunt´s and uncle´s wedding, but she takes the right to visualize it in order to piece all the parts she has together and create a whole image: "I suspect, […] I really don´t know. No one speaks of this wedding; there are no photographs" (ibid., p. 77).

Not only does Helen try to gain information from her parents, but she also looks elsewhere and takes advantage of other sources to find out more about the past. Her sister investigates and writes to a Rabbi in Yad Vashem, a Holocaust museum in Israel (cf. ibid., p. 29) and receives documents about her Jewish family (cf. ibid., p. 29). The sisters fill the gaps with the help of other sources than familial oral testimony. They search history books, contact the Red Cross and talk with other survivors and rabbis (cf. ibid., p. 34).

The girls push their parents to tell them more in order to break the silence the family has been keeping up for years. Lara insists they "'[...] have to get Mom and Dad to tell us more about what happened during the war'" (ibid., p. 159). The daughters deal with their origin, where everything started and where their own roots came to be.

The constant battle between the first and the second generation about the revealing of the past makes an identity creation of the daughters possible eventually. What goes along with this formation is the quest for a version of a story that is not necessarily considered to be accurate. Helen allows memory gaps and different versions of truth: "It's not clear what happened. But nothing is ever exactly clear. History is a card full of illusions, and we must sort through and pick the ones we wish to believe" (ibid., p. 130). Helen chooses a version of reality for herself and creates a coherent story regardless of its truth value or the inaccuracy that memory might entail. She chooses the details of her parents' experiences and the story finally takes shape. Helen also portrays her own inaccurate memory: "When I was small, maybe I was 5 or 6, [...]" (ibid., p. 11). Memory can be unreliable, in which images fall over each other and merge together (cf. ibid., p. 174). Helen is fully aware of this fact and accepts alterations of truth: "Or perhaps it's my mother who has made a few changes now, fifty years later, when she tells her daughter, to suit her own needs" (ibid., p. 243). This possibility is fully accepted by Helen and she knows she can never know what happened or retrace her parents' steps completely.

Still, the high amount of unknown gaps needs to be filled. Helen knows at one point that she: "[...] will fill this vacuum with words until I recognize them as memory " (ibid., p. 186).

The way Helen can create her own path without being disturbed by her parent's path is to create a narrative for herself. The act of writing allows her to fill the gaps with words. Although Helen does not know her mother's real name, she calls her Batya. The reader cannot know if that is in fact her real name, but the gap is filled with it and therefore Helen´s version ceases to exist.

Sometimes, Helen also invents dialogues and imagines in which language her ancestors or friends of her parents could have spoken in. She imagines their conversations and constructs again a version of the past admitting: "I don´t know if he said this. I don´t know Polish, or Yiddish, or whatever language they spoke to each other. I wasn´t there" (ibid., p. 233).

Since Helen wants to break the silence of her parents, she also tries to break up her own habit of keeping silent and tells her mother she is gay (cf. ibid., p. 256). All secrets are now disclosed. She now embraces her full identity, not in a religious sense since Helen is not very religious (cf. ibid., p. 160), but in a sense of belonging to a community. Helen argues that both sisters of the second generation found their own lives. Helen seems to be more convinced of that than Lara who still doubts the success of their quest. The reason for that could be Helen´s visible imagining of an unknown past with the help of her work of art. She accepts certain gaps, fills some by imaginative investment and projection as well as with information from other sources and unfreezes internalized images given by her parents. She finds meaning in the past by visualizing scenarios in her mind to the extent that all first generation members are a creation of hers. Batya, Kovik and Zosia mirror her version of the past and do not represent necessarily real existent people.

The form of the work represents Helen´s struggle with the past and the formulation of her own identity. Her own feelings and experiences are embedded fragmentarily within the stories of her parents´ past (cf. ibid., pp. 128-129). She actively expresses what the survivors could not and writes about their memory. The act of writing establishes a sense of autonomy: "Now I tell the story, I suppose, because it is the only way to loosen the now that has held us captive for so long" (ibid., p. 346). The uncertainty of a proper recall is blended out. The meaning is found in the transmission of knowledge and not historical truth. Especially with memoirs, authenticity is created by invention and unreliability is part of history. In the author´s note we read that the memoir is a work of nonfiction (cf. ibid., no page). The combination of survivor testimony, imaginative investment and interpretation mixed with emotions and reflections and a given context turns this memoir into a true version of reality. Since it is written post-factum, there is only needed information in the memoir, which eliminates unnecessary memories or situations. Only needed memories are used. The reader and the active presence, the author, have all the information that is needed to have a coherent story. This is exactly what Helen needs for establishing an own sense of autonomy and identity.

# 7.  Conclusion

The first generation´s traumatic experiences after World War II and the Holocaust are of extreme importance for the existence of survivor children. The trauma of Vladek´s direct trauma after the war has been elaborated and his symptoms pointed out. He is afflicted with disconnection, helplessness and isolation. He experiences a loss of control and profound changes in his behavior which does not change until his death. There is no modulation of deep anger and after his prolonged captivity he is in a constant state of alert. Anja´s suicide after her assumable PTSD concerning the Holocaust and loss of family members leads to Art´s direct trauma. He suffers from PTSD after losing her, which he portrays in a four page comic. He manages to put this trauma into a narrative. He strives for doing the same with Vladek´s past experiences, which he is vicariously and indirectly traumatized from. While Vladek does not manage to reconstruct his trauma story successfully with the involvement of emotions and reflections, Art accomplishes to keep his direct and indirect trauma separated and to find a story for both of his traumata.

In *After Long Silence* the first generation suffers from complex trauma as well. The inability to talk about it haunts them throughout the whole work. The parents emotional and fragmented utterances and the anticipation of danger accompanies them all the time.

Helen and her sister Lara are affected deeply by their parents´ trauma as well. Their parents and aunt keep silent about their past and are not able to work it through. The first generation of both works sticks to their trauma unable to find relief or calm down. At first, both implied authors and members of the second generation show little empathy concerning the traumatic past, but during their voyage of discovery they develop more and more understanding for the first generation´s inability to find language.

Art Spiegelman´s *The Complete Maus* and Helen Fremont´s *After Long Silence* present different ways of investigating the past by using different aesthetic forms.

The comic makes silence and gaps possible with the help of narrative and images. The reading of the comic turns the reader into an active participant and by performing closure in McCloud´s terms mimics the experience of trauma, which entails gaps and holes and the unspeakability of certain events as well. This duality of trauma gaps and the gutter is not presentable in Fremont´s narrative. In *After Long Silence* the reader does not get to see gaps and holes unless it is mentioned with words. The unspeakability of trauma cannot be represented without words, but it needs to be actually said, marking a paradox.

The graphic narrative enables the juxtaposition of time that makes the co-existence of present and past possible. This medium allows the simultaneousness in contrast to other aesthetic works. Spiegelman´s work is also able to portray different versions of truth at the same time. Spiegelman depicts a panel with the image of an orchestra in Auschwitz as well as one without it due to Vladek´s inability to remember the musicians. The gaps in memory and the unreliability is presented here very clearly. The portrayal of other sources as diagrams or maps is also easier to depict in a graphic narrative.

Fremont does not make use of visual material. It is more difficult to depict memory gaps or the external sources she studies to gain more information about the past as, for instance, the documents she receives from Yad Vashem. Fremont nevertheless manages to underline her parents´ trauma and her own implication in it. She underlines her mother´s inaccurate memory as well as her own by using words alone.

Both works contain two levels of time and both authors switch between them constantly.

They both are able to piece together the unknown past and find their own identity on a collective as well as individual level. Due to a sense of belonging to a group, they take part in a shared commemoration of the past. They preserve the past and, as active presences, they assume the burden of memory and become witnesses to themselves. Art Spiegelman and Helen Fremont go through a process of imaginative creation so that they invent figures, places and dialogues for their own cohesive narration. The depicted truth in both works does not necessarily have to mirror the characters in real life. What is of importance is the authors´ intention to portray their versions of truth and their act of writing.

The gaps that occur in the parents´ narratives and the holes in their memory are reminiscent of the gaps in trauma theory. In this sense, trauma and postmemory are connected to a great extent. The desire for filled gaps and a coherent reconstruction of the event is necessary for both concepts.

The overlapping of true and forged images that pop up in the victim´s mind after PTSD occurs in postmemorial work and its invention of a version of the past as well.

The second generation fills the gaps due to a internalized wish to know what happened in the past. Since the memory and narration of the first generation has its holes, their statements are unreliable. The unreliability of the trauma goes hand in hand with the unreliability of the second generation, which fills these holes by imaginative investment, creation and projection.

History and historical accuracy is not to be understood merely by correct and detailed investigations but also implies testimonial work done by survivors. The emotions, experiences and own reflections count as history as well. The two levels of unreliability do not minimize the second generation´s works on no account since not only historical facts make testimony and memory accurate.

Postmemory depicts an antagonistic intergenerational act. It involves working together as well as against each other. The first generation, unwilling to accept other stories and truths than their own due to the enormous extent of traumatization they suffer from, tends to negate the second generation´s wish to build a sense of autonomy and identity.

In both works, the second generation transforms the pain transmitted by the parents into a creative and interpretive act. It is put into narration and another context so that it restores the negative emotions felt by the children. They manage to evolve a sense of autonomy by creating a story for themselves that is different from the stories of their parents. Both authors create a post-factum identity, after having experienced meta-fictional self-reflexivity which has been put into words and into a coherent narrative. By writing an own story, the children inscribe themselves into the stories of their parents.

The horrific events of the Shoah took place numerous decades earlier and members of the first generation are dying out more and more. The topic of the Holocaust however is still discussed to this very day. Members of the second as well as third generation and people who are directly or indirectly implicated in the aftermath of the Holocaust commemorate the victims and losses of that time by participating in rituals, visiting monuments and museums. This horrendous trauma is still culturally reproduced. It would be of interest to investigate the extent to which the third generation is nowadays implicated in the aftermath of the Holocaust and to see how the transmission of trauma occurs from the second to the third generation. As long as commemorations take place and people are touched by the Holocaust´s imaginable magnitude, this topic of the Holocaust is going to occupy our minds until someday maybe the shadows of the past will no longer haunt us anymore.

# Works Cited

## Primary Sources

Fremont, Helen: *After Long Silence. A Memoir.* New York, Delta Trade Paperback 1999

Freud, Sigmund: *Jenseits des Lustprinzips.* 3. durchges. Aufl. Leipzig [et al.], Internationaler Psychoanalytischer Verlag 1923

Spiegelman, Art: *The Complete Maus.* New York, Penguin Books 2003

## Secondary Sources

Alexander, Jeffrey C.: *Toward a Theory of Cultural Trauma.* In: Alexander, Jeffrey C.: *Cultural Trauma and Collective Identity.* Berkeley, Calif. [et al.], Univ. of California Press 2004, pp. 1-30

Baer, Ulrich: *Spectral Evidence. The Photography of Trauma.* Cambridge, Mass. [et al.], MIT Press 2002

Banner, Gillian: *Holocaust Literature. Schulz, Levi, Spiegelman and the memory of the offence.* London [et al.], Mitchell 2000

Bergmann, Martin S./Jucovy, Milton E. : *Epilogue.* In: Bergmann, Martin S. (ed.)/Jucovy, Milton E.: *Generations of the Holocaust.* New York, Basic Books 1982, pp. 311-316

Bergmann, Maria V.: *Thoughts on Superego Pathology of Survivors and Their Children.* In: Bergmann, Martin S. (ed.)/Jucovy, Milton E.: *Generations of the Holocaust.* New York, Basic Books 1982, pp. 287-309

Berlatsky, Eric: *Memory as Forgetting: The Problem of the Postmodern in Kundera´s The Book of Laughter and Spiegelman´s Maus.* In: Cultural Critique, Volume 55, 2003, pp. 101-151

Caruth, Cathy: *Unclaimed Experience. Trauma, Narrative, and History.* Baltimore, Md. [et al.], Johns Hopkins Univ. Press 1996

Chute, Hillary: *Comics as Literature? Reading Graphic Narrative.* In: PMLA, Volume 123, Number 2, 2008, pp. 452-465

Danieli, Yael: *Confronting the Unimaginable. Psychotherapist's Reactions to Victims of the Nazi Holocaust.* In: Wilson (ed.) [et al.]: *Human Adaptation to Extreme Stress. From the Holocaust to Vietnam.* New York [et al.], Plenum Pr. 1988, pp. 219-238

Doherty, Thomas: *Art Spiegelman's Maus: Graphic Art and the Holocaust.* In: American Literature, Write Now: American Literature in 1980's and 1990's. Volume 68, Number 1, 1996, pp. 69-84

Ehman, Paul: *Three Classes of Nonverbal Behavior.* In: Von Raffler-Engel, Walburga (ed.): *Aspects of Nonverbal Communication,* Lisse, Swets and Zeitlinger 1980, pp. 89-103

Eisner, Will: *Graphic Storytelling and Visual Narrative. Principles and Practices from the Legendary Cartoonist.* New York [et al.], W. W. Norton 2008

Elmwood, Victoria A.: *Happy, Happy Ever After: The Transformation of Trauma Between the Generations in Art Spiegelman's Maus: A Survivor's Tale.* In: Biography Volume 27, Number 4, 2004, pp. 691-720

Epstein, Helen: *Die Kinder des Holocaust. Gespräche mit Söhnen und Töchtern von Überlebenden.* Aus dem Engl übers., München, Verlag C.H. Beck 1987

Evers, Florian: *Vexierbilder des Holocaust. Ein Versuch zum historischen Trauma in der Populärkultur.* Band 4, Berlin [et al.], LIT 2001

Felman, Shoshana: *Camus' The Plague, or a Monument to Witnessing.* In: Felman/Laub: *Testimony. Crises of Witnessing in Literature, Psychoanalysis, and History.* New York [et al.] Routledge 1992, pp. 93-119

Figley, Charles R: *Foreword.* In: Wilson (ed.) [et al.]: *Human Adaptation to Extreme Stress. From the Holocaust to Vietnam.* New York [et al.], Plenum Press 1988, pp. ix-xi

Fine, Ellen S.: *The Absent Memory: The Act of Writing in Post-Holocaust French Literature.* In: Lang, Berel (ed.): *Writing and the Holocaust.* New York [et al.], Holmes & Meier 1988, pp. 41-57

Fischer, Gottfried: *Neue Wege aus dem Trauma. Erste Hilfe bei schweren seelischen Belastungen.* 6. Aufl., Düsseldorf, Patmos 2008

Greenberg, Judith: *The Echo of Trauma and the Trauma of Echo.* In: American Imago Volume 55, Number 3, 1998, pp. 319-347

Herman, Judith: *Trauma and Recovery. The Aftermath of Violence – from Domestic Abuse to Political Terror.* New York, Basic Book 1997

Hirsch, Joshua. *Afterimage. Film, Trauma, and the Holocaust.* Philadelphia, Pa. Temple Univ. Press 2004

Hirsch, Marianne: *The Generation of Postmemory. Writing and Visual Culture After the Holocaust.* New York [et al.], Columbia University Press 2012

Hoffman, Eva: *After such Knowledge, Memory, History, and the Legacy of the Holocaust.* New York, PublicAffairs 2004

Kahana, Eva/Kahana, Boaz/Harel, Zev/Rosner, Tena: *Coping with extreme Trauma.* In: Wilson (ed.) [et al.]: *Human Adaptation to Extreme Stress. From the Holocaust to Vietnam.* New York [et al.], Plenum Pr. 1988, pp. 55-73

Kahana, Boaz/Harel, Zev/Kahana, Eva: *Predictors of Psychological Well-Being among Survivors of the Holocaust.* In: Wilson (ed.) [et al.]: *Human Adaptation to Extreme Stress. From the Holocaust to Vietnam.* New York [et al.], Plenum Pr. 1988, pp. 171-192

Kaplan, Elizabeth Ann: *Trauma Culture. The Politics of Terror and Loss in Media and Literature.* New Brunswick [et al.], Rutgers Univ. Press 2005

Kapust, Antje : *Aussöhnung mit der Fremdheit des Traumas.* In: Karger, André (ed.): *Vergessen, vergelten, vergeben, versöhnen? Weiterleben mit dem Trauma.* Band 30, Göttingen [et al.], Vandenhoeck & Ruprecht 2012, pp. 97-113

Kestenberg, Judith S.: *A Metapsychological Assessment Based on Analysis of a Survivor's Child.* In: Bergmann, Martin S. (ed.)/Jucovy, Milton E.: *Generations of the Holocaust.* New York, Basic Books 1982, pp. 137-158

Kestenberg, Judith S./Kestenberg, Milton: *The Background of the Study.* In: Bergmann, Martin S. (ed.)/Jucovy, Milton E.: *Generations of the Holocaust.* New York, Basic Books 1982, pp. 33-45

Kestenberg, Judith S.: *Survivor Parents and Their Children.* In: Bergmann, Martin S. (ed.)/Jucovy, Milton E.: *Generations of the Holocaust.* New York, Basic Books 1982, pp. 83-102

Kirmayer, Laurence J./Gone, Joseph P./Moses, Joshua: *Rethinking Historical Trauma.* In: Transcultural Psychiatry, Volume 53, Number 3, 2014 pp. 299-319

Klein-Parker, Fran: *Dominant Attitudes of Adult Children of Holocaust Survivors toward Their Parents.* In: Wilson (ed.) [et al.]: *Human Adaptation to Extreme Stress. From the Holocaust to Vietnam.* New York [et al.], Plenum Pr. 1988, pp. 193-218

LaCapra, Dominick: *Representing the Holocaust. History, Theory, Trauma.* Ithaca [et al.], Cornell Univ. Press 1994

LaCapra, Dominick: *Writing History, Writing Trauma.* Baltimore, Md. [et al.], John Hopkins Univ. Press 2001

Lang, Berel: *Holocaust Representation. Art within the Limits of History and Ethics.* Baltimore [et al.], John Hopkins Univ. Press, 2000

Laub, Dori. *An Event Without a Witness: Truth, Testimony and Survival.* In: Felman/Laub: *Testimony. Crises of Witnessing in Literature, Psychoanalysis, and History.* New York [et al.] Routledge 1992, pp. 75-92

Laub, Dori: *Bearing Witness, or the Vicissitudes of Listening.* In: Felman/Laub: *Testimony. Crises of Witnessing in Literature, Psychoanalysis, and History.* New York [et al.] Routledge 1992, pp. 57-74

Lifton, Robert J: *Understanding the Traumatized Self. Imagery, Symbolization, and Transformation.* In: Wilson (ed.) [et al.]: *Human Adaptation to Extreme Stress. From the Holocaust to Vietnam.* New York [et al.], Plenum Pr. 1988, pp. 7-31

Mandaville, Alison: *Tailing Violence: Comic Narrative, Gender and the Father-Tale in Art Spiegelman´s Maus.* In: Critical Pacific Coast Philology, Volume 44, Number 2, 2009, p. 216-248

McCloud, Scott: *Understanding Comics.* [*The Invisible Art*]. 1. HarperPerennial ed. New York, Morrow 1994

McGlothlin, Erin: *"When time stands still": Traumatic Immediacy and Narrative Organization in Art Spiegelman´s Maus and In the Shadow of No Towers.* In: Baskind, S./Omer-Sherman, R.: *The Jewish Graphic Novel. Critical Approaches.* New Brunswick [et al.] Rutgers Univ. Press 2008, pp. 94-110

Mulman, Lisa Naomi: *A Tale of Two Mice: Graphic Representations of the Jew in Holocaust Narrative.* In: Baskind, S. (ed.)/Omer-Sherman, R.: *The Jewish Graphic Novel. Critical Approaches.* New Brunswick [et al.] Rutgers Univ. Press 2008 pp. 85-93

Rothe, Anne: *Popular Trauma Culture. Selling the Pain of Others in the Mass Media*. New Brunswick [et al.], Rurgers Univ. Press 2011

Schmidtgall, Thomas: *Traumatische Erfahrung im Mediengedächtnis. Zur Struktur und interkulturellen Rezeption fiktionaler Darstellungen des 11. September 2001 in Deutschland, Frankreich und Spanien*. Würzburg, Königshausen & Neumann 2014

Silbermann, Alphons: *The Way Toward a Visual Culture: Comics and Comic Films*. In: Silbermann, Alphons (ed.)/Dyroff, H.-D.: *Comics and Visual Culture. Research Studies from 10 Countries*. München [et al.] Saur 1986, pp. 11-28

Spiegelman, Art: *MetaMaus. [Art Spiegelman look inside a modern classic, MAUS + The complete MAUS, a hyperlinked DVD of MAUS with an in-depth archive of audio interviews with his father, photos, notebooks, drawings, essays and more]*. London, Viking 2011

White, Sheila J. : *Nonverbal Antecedents to Language Functioning: A Model and its Relevance for the Deaf*. In: Key, Mary Ritchie (ed.): *Nonverbal Communication Today. Current Research*, Berlin, Mouton 1982, pp. 233-242

Wigand, Rolf T.: *Toward a more Visual Culture Through Comics*. In: Silbermann, Alphons (ed.)/Dyroff, H.-D.: *Comics and Visual Culture. Research Studies from 10 Countries*. München [et al.] Saur 1986, pp. 28-62

Williams, Tom: *Diagnosis and Treatment of Survivor Guilt: The Bad Penny Syndrome*. In: Wilson (ed.) [et al.]: *Human Adaptation to Extreme Stress. From the Holocaust to Vietnam*. New York [et al.], Plenum Pr. 1988, pp. 319-336

Young, James Edward. *Beschreiben des Holocaust. Darstellung und Folgen der Interpretation*. 1. Aufl., Frankfurt am Main. Jüd. Verl., 1992

Young, James Edward: *The Holocaust as Vicarious Past: Art Spiegelman´s Maus and the Afterimages of History*. In: Critical Inquiry, Volume 24, Number 3, 1998, pp. 666-699

Young, James Edward: *Toward a Received History of the Holocaust*. In: History and Theory, Volume 36, 1997, pp. 21-43

Zeitlin, Froma I. *The Vicarious Witness. Belated Memory and Authorial Presence in Recent Holocaust Literature.* In: History & Memory, Volume 10, Number 2, 1998, pp. 5-42